Provence of

ALAIN DUCASSE

For Gwenaelle

© 2000 Assouline Publishing, Inc. for the present edition
First published by Editions Assouline, Paris

Assouline Publishing, Inc.
601 West 26ᵗʰ Street
18ᵗʰ floor
New York, NY 10001
USA

www.assouline.com

ISBN : 2 84323 247 3

Translated from the French by Louise Guiney
Front cover: Ermel Vialet
Back cover image: Laziz Hamani

Printed in Italy

Provence of

ALAIN DUCASSE

ASSOULINE

Table of contents

• • •

All the prices mentioned are based on the currency exchange of 7.50 F on the US dollar.

The French region of Provence seems, curiously, to suffer from a fundamental misunderstanding. People expect it to embody absolutes—endlessly azure skies, palm trees, the Riviera, a dolce vita for the wealthy . . . all of which is there, of course.

But to me Provence is something very different from this superficial indolence. Almost the exact opposite, in fact. And this is what I have always tried to suggest through my cuisine, to develop in my dishes: Provence as a secret land, simple and good.

Cruising the boulevards in a fancy convertible, one elbow draped casually over the doorframe, is not the way to do it. You have to take the back roads. A "back road," according to the dictionary, is "a distinctive type, shorter than a main road, leading where no main road goes." In my Provence notebooks you'll find addresses that have become famous, and rightly so, but ones that have often managed to remain secret, simple. And good. They are precarious establishments that sometimes disappear by the time a new season opens. I invite you to leaf through these notebooks the way I might, traveling the roads of Provence. With love, discretion and simplicity. When you do, you'll receive the blessings of that other Provence. Hidden and worthy, desirable and subtly satisfying.

OLIVE OIL

If you're interested in getting to know me, follow the olive oil trail and you'll discover the thread leading straight to the heart of my cuisine.

Of course I use it for cooking, for sautéing and deep-frying, but there's more to olive oil than that. It's not just a fabulous helpmate, it's something I feel deep inside—cultural roots. The Greeks, the Mediterranean, Provence . . . Behind this winding golden thread lie millennia of civilization, bounty, and beauty. When I open a bottle of olive oil, I can't help thinking of all that.

Follow my example and make olive oil your helpmate. Like salt and pepper, it is something you should always have on hand. Better yet, consider diversifying your assets: use different types for fish, salad, meat, and stews.

Logically, every dish calls for a different type of olive oil.

Olive Trees,
Van Gogh,
1889.

My favorite olive oils

Nyons (Drôme). ✱ Coopérative du Nyonsais, Place Olivier-de-Serres (04.75.26.03.44) ✱ Stop here for a powerful olive oil—and the superb countryside. La Route des Baronnies, exit Nyons on D538 direction Buis-les-Baronnies via Miravel-aux-Baronnies, then D71 via Merindol-les-Oliviers and Mollans-sur-Ouvèze.

Lauris (Vaucluse). ✱ Boudoire, Frères Merindol, Les Pilon-Ouest (04.90.72.80.48) ✱ Made with a relatively rare olive, *la blanquette*.

Saint-Saturnin-les-Apt (Vaucluse). ✱ Moulin à Huile Jullien, 1 Rue Albert-Tronchet (04.90.75.45.80) ✱ Subtle and untamed, ideal with fish.

Arles (Bouches-du-Rhône). ✱ Huiles Jamard, 46 Rue des Arènes (04.90.49.70.73) ✱ A shop where you can sample different types of various origins. Extend your pleasure at the nearby restaurant, L'Entrevue (Le Méjan, 23 Quai Marx Dormoy, 04.90.93.37.28), featuring a menu based on olive oil (150 F – $20).

Auriol (Bouches-du-Rhône). ✱ Moulin Margier-Aubert, Quai de l'Huveaune (04.42.04.74.09) ✱ Jean-François Margier: award-winning and much sought-after olive oil.

Lançon-de-Provence (Bouches-du-Rhône). ✱ Château Virant, via La Route de La Fare, at Saint-Chamas (04.90.42.44.47) ✱ Robert Cheylan: a major effort to market different types of olive oil (blends and pure types).

Maussane (Bouches-du-Rhône). ✱ Coopérative Oléicole, M. Cornille, Rue C.-Rieu (04.90.54.32.37) ✱ Fine fruity bouquet, highly reputed.

Mouriès (Bouches-du-Rhône). The olive-oil capital of France and the scene, in mid-September, of the Green Olive Festival (04.90.47.56.58). Saturday: flea market. Sunday: blessing of the groves and samplings of olive oil in every guise—*fougasses* and *pompes* (local breads), oils.

Le Beausset (Var), via N8. ✱ Domaine de Souviou (04.94.90.57.63) ✱ Ask for Serge Cagnolari.

Flayosc (Var). ✱ Moulin du Flayosquet, Hameau du Flayosquet (04.94.70.41.45). Shop at 2 Place Brémont (04.94.7043.52) ✱ Also ✱ Max Doléatto ✱ for oil from the Figanières Plain.

Manosque (Alpes-de-Haute-Provence). ✱ Moulin de l'Olivette, Place Olivette (04.92.72.00.99) ✱

Les Mées (Alpes-de-Haute-Provence). ✱ Moulin des Pénitents, Coopérative Oléicole du Plan et des Mées, Parc d'Activités La Chauchière (04.92.34.07.67) ✱ Nothing could be better for appreciating this olive oil to the fullest than a short stroll through the superb olive grove (containing 6,000 trees) located above the cooperative on a small road near the canal. Survey the countryside, fill your lungs with fresh air, and sample some olive oil straight from the spoon. Unforgettable.

Two vintages are currently available, Olea Nostra (105 F – $14) and Olea Diva (120 F – $16). Eric Verdier's comment: "Oil from the Les Mées Cooperative, based on the *aglandou* olive, is a delicate, peppery oil with a full-bodied texture accented by tropical-fruit accents (primarily banana) and organic notes of straw, bay leaf, and green tomato." In the kitchen, this oil goes well with lamb, pork chops, *soupe au pistou*, warm bean salad with sherry vinegar, lentils (*du Puy* variety), and Moroccan specialties.

Menton (Alpes-Maritimes). ✱ Maurice Lottier, 102 Avenue des Acacias (04.93.35.79.15) ✱

Nice (Alpes-Maritimes). ✱ Maison Alziari, 14 Rue Saint François de Paule (04.93.85.76.92) ✱ A spectacular shop, with its huge vats, signet bottles and, of course, the very mild and fruity oil *maison*. Numerous related products, including *tapenade* and olives. Shipment by mail on request.

Peillon (Alpes-Maritimes). ✱ Le Moulin de Roger Guido, Quartier Sainte Thècle (04.93.91.24.40) ✱

Sclos-de-Contes (Alpes-Maritimes). ✱ Joël Gambiez, Quartier Riole (04.93.79.03.02) ✱ Light, very fruity oil.

Tourettes-sur-Loup (Alpes-Maritimes). ✱ Edith and Pierre Poussou, 966 Route des Valettes (04.93.24.12.81) ✱ Limited production; the oil used at Monaco's Le Louis XV restaurant.

La Trinité (Alpes-Maritimes). ✱ Lessatini Yves & Fils, 77 Vieux Chemin (04.93.54.33.41) ✱ Oil made of olives from Nice, Catalonia, etc. An extraordinary product!

A new geography of taste

Mane (Alpes-de-Haute-Provence). Olive oil is a mysterious continent we explore with the tip of a spoon. It can be good or less good . . . but that's only the beginning. Olive oil resembles wine in that quality depends on the type of olives, the year in which they were harvested, the soil in which they were grown. Got it?

The next step is to delve into a fantastic medley of flavors featuring accents as different as pepper, salt, fresh almond, artichoke, and mown hay.

This is where Eric Verdier comes in.

Verdier works with Oliviers & Co., a leading olive-oil supplier founded by Olivier Baussan. Every year, this company "selects" its olive oils from the entire Mediterranean basin, "collects" vintages, and packs them in elegant little metal tins. For the 1999 harvest, only 22 olive oils—from Tuscany, Andalusia, Latium, Ombria, Istria, the Peloponnesus peninsula, Crete, Galilee, and Provence—made the cut. This selectivity has created a whole new geography of taste: bountiful, universal, and highly specialized. Here is a breadth of vision inviting us to learn more about (and to hone) the tastes we associate with salads, fish, and so on.

The address: ✷ Oliviers & Co., Avenue Burlière, Mane (04.92.70.48.20) ✷ Branches in Paris (Rue Montorgueil, Rue Saint-Louis-en-l'Isle, Rue de Buci), Cannes (Rue Macé), and Strasbourg (Rue Miroir). Toll-free number for direct orders: 0800.03.28.96.

My recipe for tapenade

1 lb. black Mediterranean olives,
1 clove garlic, 2 salted anchovy fillets,
basil leaves, 1 cup olive oil

* Remove pits from olives. * Peel garlic clove, cut into 4 slices,
and discard green inner sprout. * Cut anchovy fillets
into small pieces, remove bones, rinse.
* Chop the basil. Place all ingredients in blender container
and blend while gradually adding the olive oil
until a creamy mixture is obtained.

If the tapenade will not be used immediately, pour
into a jar, cover with olive oil, and refrigerate. Tapenade
is an ideal accompaniment for raw vegetables and can also
be used as a canapé spread or a garnish for salads,
grilled fish, or potatoes.

TOMATOES

In my kitchen, the tomato is like a sun, with olive oil for rays.
Sadly, I have often had to endure terrible, long-lasting eclipses.
Tomatoes are now available everywhere at every season of the year,
but (as you may have guessed) they are not always the real,
flavorful product I'm looking for. The unnaturally round, red,
firm, out-of-season tomato is often completely tasteless.
It puts on a good show but can't deliver the goods.

* **How do you recognize a good tomato?** You have to trust your
own sense of taste, which should be trained and developed.
Basically, a good tomato will offer an appealing balance
between acidity and sweetness. It should also be juicy,
yet firm. You're not going to find it just anywhere. You have
to track it down, discover its lair, and smoke it out.
The tomato that rewards your search isn't necessarily
rare—there are over 4,500 **varieties** in an incredible range
of shapes and colors (white, green, black).

* **Bear in mind that Provençal tomatoes are seasonal:
between August 15th and September 15th.** The tomato,
the quintessential vegetable of Provence, wasn't introduced   into
the region until the late 18th century. It's used in the simplest
dishes (tomato salad, for example), and, in sunny climes, it also
turns up in tomato purée, ratatouille, stuffed tomatoes, tomato
timbale, tomatoes à la Provençale. Although the development of new
varieties has blurred the distinctiveness of the Provençal tomato, there
have been gains in quality and choice, as demonstrated by the fabulous
work conducted at the Jardin des Olivades in Ollioules.

✳ Where to find tomatoes

Avignon (Vaucluse). ✳ Christian Etienne's restaurant at 10 Rue de Mons (04.90.86.16.50)✳ has an entire menu (300 F – $40) devoted to the tomato—tomato tartare with basil, tomato fondant with saffron, sautéed fillets of mullet, slices of *romas* with olives, braised *panoufs* of lamb with dreied tomato, goat cheese in tomato *tapenade,* green-tomato pie.

Carpentras (Vaucluse). ✳ Open Market (Friday mornings)✳ The stall at 93 Avenue Jean Jaurès offers tomato slips for transplanting, fresh tomatoes of every variety, and also thyme, peppermint, melons, citronella.

Velleron (Vaucluse). ✳ Open Market (late afternoons, daily except Sundays)✳ One of the most interesting displays in the region. A farmer's market open only to growers who harvest their produce the same day. Tomatoes are everywhere, especially on the right at the end of the aisle, along with the tiny vegetables grown by a farm woman from Jonquerettes.

Mouries (Bouches-du-Rhône). ✳ Brunette Caramella (grower), Chemin des Poissonniers (04.90.47.59.40)✳ produces old-fashioned vegetables and classic tomatoes. Her display of vegetables is worth a visit.

Ollioules (Var). Le Jardin des Olivades, Daniel and Denise Vuillon (growers). Farm produce, seasonal fruits and vegetables, special gourmet varieties. ✳ Les Olivades shop, Quartier Quiez, between Continent and the La Seyne railway station, opposite McDonald's (04.94.30.03.13, open afternoons on Mondays, Wednesdays, Thursdays, and Fridays from 2:30 to 7:00 P.M., Saturday mornings from 9 A.M. to noon)✳ Some twenty varieties of tomato available, some with evocative names such as evergreen, reine de Sainte-Marthe, joie de la table, rose de Berne, délicieuse de Morny, beefsteak, montfavet, la russe, andine cornue, yellow Saint-Vincent, white beauty, brandywine.

A consumer panel awarded first place to the rose de Berne variety for taste, but the evergreen, andine cornue, and Crimean black also have their fans. Plan on spending about 10 F per pound ($1.40). Slips for transplanting (in season) at 5 F ($.75) apiece.

Antibes (Alpes-Maritimes). ✳ Open Market, Cours Masséna (Tuesdays, Fridays, Saturdays, Sundays)✳ Fine selection in the center of the market at a number of stalls, especially Madame Louise's.

Cagnes (Alpes-Maritimes). ✳ Open Market, Cité Marchande, Rue de l'Eglise and Rue du Marché✳ Fruits and vegetables from Madame Benetto.

Grasse (Alpes-Maritimes). ✳ Produce shop, Nature Dis, 57 Boulevard Marcel Pagnol (04.92.42.48.48)✳ Below the town you'll find one of the largest organic-produce suppliers on the Côte d'Azur (or even Italy and Corsica), with a continuous supply and a vast selection.

Menton (Alpes-Maritimes). ✳ Open Market, municipal marketplace (daily)✳ Be sure to stop at Philippe Catananzi's stall. It's easy to find, right next to the "*bord de mer*" entrance. Catananzi has Menton lemons, of course, and also fine local tomatoes and all the locally-grown fruits and vegetables.

Nice (Alpes-Maritimes). ✳ Open Market, Cours Saleya✳ The best small growers are located on Place Gautier, to the left. One of the very finest is Madame Flavio. The best day? Saturday. But the market's open daily, except Mondays.

Nice (Alpes-Maritimes). ✳ The Zucca Magica restaurant, 4-bis Quai Papacio (04.93.56.25.27, closed Sundays)✳ A vegetarian restaurant dedicated to the cult of vegetables in every guise: timbales *au gratin,* pizzetta featuring tomato and zucchini. Menu (for lunch only): 80 F ($11); *à la carte:* 150 F ($20).

My recipe for tomato salad with tomato vinaigrette

4 beefsteak tomatoes, 1 belle russe tomato, 2 large mild onions,
2 tablespoons flat parsley leaves, 2 tablespoons mild wine vinegar,
5 tablespoons extra-virgin olive oil, 2 pinches fine salt,
1 pinch "fleur de sel" salt, pepper (5 turns of the grinder),
1 small very ripe tomato for its juice.

* The night before, peel the small tomato and squeeze it through
a strainer to collect the pulp and juice. * Add 2 tablespoons olive oil
and a dash of wine vinegar, cover with plastic wrap and refrigerate.

* The next day, all you need to do is cut the other tomatoes into
round slices about 1 inch thick and the onions into thin slices.

* Make a vinaigrette in the usual way, using the olive oil, remaining
vinegar, salt and pepper. Add the tomato juice-pulp preparation
on serving plates and cover with the tomato vinaigrette. Serve.

An olive oil: I have my favorite oil and my favorite supplier.
Saint-Catherine olive oil produced by Pierre and Edith Poussou
at Tourettes-sur-Loup (Alpes-Maritimes), 966 Route des Valettes
(04.93.24.12.81). This oil has an extraordinarily fruity bouquet with
accents of artichoke, hazelnut, and dry almond, which blend perfectly
with tomatoes.

A book: "Tomate", by Lindsay and Patrick Milanowski
(Editions du Chêne), fantastically knowledgeable and enthusiastic
on the subject of food.

A festival: every year the Jardin des Olivades in Ollioules (Var)
organizes a Tomato Festival, held on the last Saturday in July
(04.94.30.03.13).

* * *

My recipe for tomato sauce

(A very simple tomato sauce base, or passato, to "get through the winter")

13 lbs. firm, ripe tomatoes (Italian plum-type)

10 half-quart mason jars, 1 vegetable mill

* Cut the tomatoes in half lengthwise.

* Place them in a large pot and cover with cold water.

* Do not season. Seasonings are added when the passato is used.

* Slowly raise heat under the pot to the boiling point, stirring from time to time. * The tomatoes are cooked when they begin to foam.

 * Meanwhile, wash and scald the jars. * Put the cooked tomatoes through the vegetable mill (large holes). * Allow to cool and then fill jars to just under the rim. * Seal jars hermetically. Wrap jars in cloth to prevent breakage during sterilization. * Place the jars in a large pot filled with hot water. * Bring rapidly to the boil and continue boiling for 35 minutes. * Allow the jars to cool slowly in the water in order to guarantee an air-tight seal. * Store the jars in a cool spot. When the jars are opened, any unused sauce may be covered with olive oil and the opened jar stored in the refrigerator (maximum 3 days).

"I love tomato salad with tomato vinaigrette,
because you get to have it both ways."

TRUFFLES

There's something grotesque about truffles. When you peel away their outside
  membrane, they look like clenched fists, concentrated energy,
    suppressed fury, coiled nature ready to spring.
The most striking thing about truffles is their aroma. Although "aroma"
  is perhaps not quite the right word—too timid, too polite.
  Let's say "smell." Their overwhelming smell. Explosive. A good whiff
    of this alien planet suggests a whole universe of fragrances:
  mushrooms, forests, leaves, humus. So complex and so intense
    you're tempted to say "it's truffle" the way you'd say "it's nighttime".
Truffles cannot be cultivated or reproduced at will: they arise from
a mysterious continent that drifts hither and yon beneath the earth, veering
suddenly, disappearing capriciously-because of a crumbling wall,
  a summer that's too dry or too wet.
In the kitchen, the great thing about truffles is the unique quality they
add to certain dishes, pulling things together and subtly enhancing them.
Truffles are superstars, with price tags to match.
    But don't let that stop you. It only takes an ounce or two
to transform a dish of pasta, poultry, or game. To tell the truth,
  truffles are the hallmark of a gastronomy that's understated, low key.
The note they add is so crystalline and pure, the rest of the ingredients
have only to follow its lead with humility—the humility of the truly
    discriminating, ensuring that nothing is ever overdone.
Nature always does things right, which is why the **white summer truffle**
  opens the season. You have to wait for November to taste **the fabulous**
white Alba truffle from Italy. Later in November comes **the black truffle**
from France's Périgord region (although most now actually come from
  throughout the southwest of France), but the black truffle is really
    at its best between mid-January and the end of February.

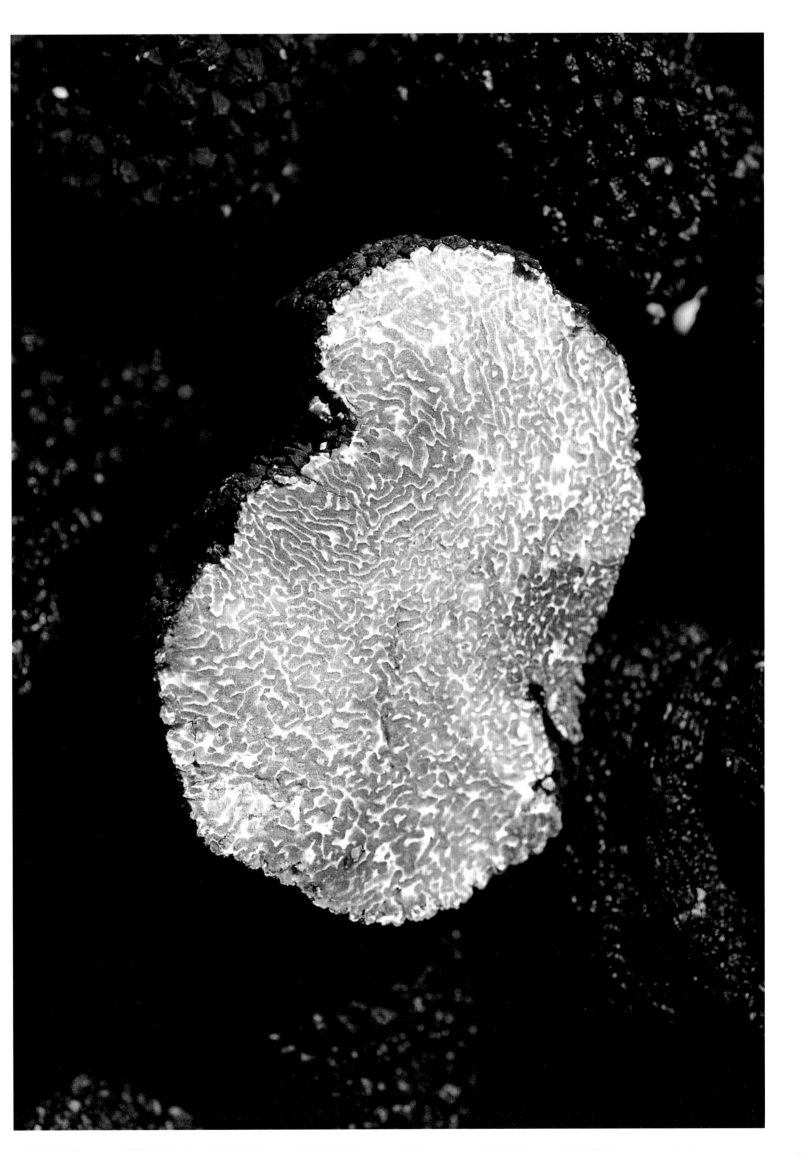

Where to find truffles

* * *

Mondragon (Drôme). ✳La Beaugravière, Quai du Pont-Neuf (04.90.40.82.54)✳ Guy Jullien not only offers the finest selection in the world of Côtes-du-Rhône wines (his cellar is truly phenomenal), but he's also a truffle specialist (willing to ship by express mail if necessary), cooking (in season) a truffle menu that's simplicity itself.

He also has a few rooms for those who want to prolong the pleasure of their visit. Meals from 130 to 400 F ($17–53), rooms from 265 to 395 F ($35–53).

Carpentras (Vaucluse). Every Friday, with a blast on his whistle, the *garde champêtre* signals opening time for this up-dated traditional market featuring merchant guilds, goods sold from burlap sacks. ✳Opens about 8 A.M., Place Aristide Briand, in front of the Café de l'Univers.

Monteux (Vaucluse). ✳La Truffe du Lubéron, la Quinsonne (04.90.61.04.25)✳ Dominique Jaumard ships truffles harvested from his own estate within 24 hours throughout France.

Richeranches (Vaucluse). ✳The largest truffle market in France, open Saturday mornings from 8 A.M. You can't miss the market—it runs along the main street of town, around the two cafés✳ Worth a visit. Unpretentious and quite fascinating.

Saint-Didier (Vaucluse). ✳Gilbert Esperon, Route du Beaucet (04.90.66.01.33)✳ One of the region's specialists. Ships within 48 hours.

Ampus (Var). ✳Maison de la Truffe (by the Town Hall, 04.94.70.97.11)✳ On the La Roche-Aiguille geological site, an old, recently restored country house dedicated to the cult of these black diamonds.

Lorgues (Var). ✳La Truffe et le Vin, Route de Vidauban (04.94.85.93.93)✳ The Truffle Emperor—a.k.a. Bruno—expanded his restaurant to include a shop marketing truffles in all of their diversity. Black, white, in oil, in cream, etc.

Rougiers (Var). ✳Hugou Dumas (04.94.80.45.95)✳ One of the most respected outlets in the area.

Plateau de Sault (Alpes-de-Haute-Provence). ✳During truffle season, the Agence Provence Grandeur Nature, 203 Rue Oscar Roulet at Robion (04.90.76.68.27)✳ organizes home-stays featuring various truffle-linked activities at farm-inns on the Plateau de Sault. Guests can go truffling with dogs bred and trained by the owners, help out in the kitchen, hike, tour markets and wine cellars.

Truffles in the kitchen, La Bastide de Moustiers
(Moustiers-Sainte-Marie) ~7

FLAVORS OF PROVENCE

• The taste of zucchini blossoms

The man to whom the "Grand Chevalier of Zucchini Blossoms" ribbon should be awarded is Jacques Maximin, no doubt about it.
Back in the 1970s, Provençal cuisine was already making its mark, to be sure, executed with determination and talent; but there were no stunning coups equal to truffle soup à la VGE, mashed potatoes à la Robuchon, lobster with vanilla, water-based sauce. The required coup was finally achieved by Maximin (then at the Negresco in Nice), with his stuffed zucchini blossoms. Thus did an already famous chef earn final consecration—along with the blossom of this modest vegetable. Modest, yes. And yet, **there is nothing more vulnerable than a zucchini blossom.** Zucchini blossoms belong in the category of nervous Nellies (like omble chevalier, the crawfish, and angelica) that shrink in horror as soon as they sense a pepper mill looming above them. Zucchini blossoms will allow themselves to be stuffed, but only by hands that are gentle and understanding.

The city of Nice takes considerable pride in being the capital of the zucchini blossom, a sentiment further enhanced by the complacent knowledge that these delicate flowers do not travel well.

The best time of year? The high season is May 15th to July 15th. Later, the weather often turns too hot.
How to select them? Zucchini blossoms are now available yearlong, but avoid them when they're too pretty and fragile-looking: appearances can be deceiving. Choose them when they're firm and crisp.
How to handle them: Handle gently (they should even be protected from their own leaves) and combine only with mild flavors, such as citronella, coriander, and shellfish.

My recipe for zucchini stuffed with zucchini

4 small round zucchini, 2 large green zucchini, 4 white onions,
1 bunch flat parsley, 1 clove garlic, 1 cup chicken broth,
1 tablespoon ricotta, 1 tablespoon parmesan, 1 tablespoon pine nuts,
4 tablespoons olive oil, and salt and pepper.

* Wash the round zucchini, slice 1/3 off the tops, remove pulp and
seeds. * Salt and pepper the interior and "caps," reverse
on a rack to drain. * Wash and chop the unpeeled large zucchini.
* Peel and chop the onions. * Heat half of the olive oil
in a sauté pan, add the onions, chopped zucchini, salt, pepper.
Sauté quickly over a high flame.
* Grill the pine nuts for 2 minutes in an open pan over
a high flame. * Chop, using a knife, and combine with the sautéed
zucchini and onions. Chop the garlic and add.
* Add the ricotta, parmesan, and parsley.
* Fill the round zucchini shells with this mixture, place them
in an ovenproof pan, cover with the caps, and glaze with
a splash of olive oil. * Pour a little chicken broth over
the stuffed zucchini and bake for 20 minutes, basting frequently.

* * *

• The taste of eggplant

Eggplant can be depressing. At least to the people who grow it.
They rise at the crack of dawn, work until they drop, water the
fields, prune, fertilize, tend, harvest, pack, affix papers and labels—
and all for a pittance: 30 to 35 cents per pound at the farm,
20 cents of which is spent on packaging. When you go into rhapsodies
over the eggplant, their response is a litany of dire complaint.

The market is barely surviving, and suffers from over-production. Growers continuously seek varieties giving even higher rates of production . . . and the vicious circle goes on. The Avignon eggplant sold for twice the current price just 10 years ago. It was a fine specimen, and production was ample in terms of demand. Since then, a mad race has been heading straight into a brick wall. The only hope is to call a halt and aim for improved quality, as has been done with certain vegetables such as the Ollioules tomato. Meanwhile, however, there's nothing to do but grit the teeth, rise at the crack of dawn, etc., etc. And yet, the eggplant thrives in Avignon and the surrounding region, requiring nothing more complicated than heat, fresh air, and moisture. But all things are relative. Too much of anything spells the end of everything. For the time being, eggplant producers are still looking for a way out and shifting (very) slowly towards more natural (organic) methods, waiting for better times and decent prices.

A hint from Philippe Catanami, a pillar of the market at Menton (Alpes-Maritimes): the best eggplants have dark, lustrous skin and a bright green stem. Eggplant stored for two days under refrigeration loses its luster. The best eggplant sells for about 8 F per pound ($ 1.10).

www.lesprimeursdumistral.com.
Tomatoes, eggplants, olive oil:
hints on buying and preparation . . .

My recipe for eggplant caviar
2 lbs. eggplant, 1/2 cup olive oil, juice of 1 lemon,
salt, white pepper (ground), 3 minced spring onions
* Preheat oven to 350° F. * Cut the unpeeled eggplant in halves lengthwise and make several slashes in the pulp. * Salt the cut side of the eggplant halves, rub with oil. * Place in ovenproof pan and bake for approximately 45 minutes.

" While drifting and dreaming, you could reconstruct
your whole life around odors, aromas, and fragrances. "

* Use a spoon to scoop the pulp out of the baked eggplant, mash with a fork, and allow to drain for a few minutes.

* Add the lemon juice, finely chopped spring onions, salt and pepper.

* Blend well, gradually adding olive oil to form an emulsion.

* Cool thoroughly and spread on canapés that have been lightly rubbed with garlic.

* * *

• The taste of Solliès figs

It's not that history repeats itself. It's just that some things fall into oblivion and then reappear, a rule proved by the Solliès-Pont (Toulon) fig. If it hadn't been for a certain stream, this variety would have disappeared from the region forever, remembered only with vague nostalgia. Legend has it that late in the nineteenth century, when the Solliès fig had been largely supplanted by cherries, the grandfather of Jules Rimbaud (former mayor, deceased in 1985) discovered a small fig tree by the stream running through the hamlet of La Tour. He dug it up and transplanted it onto his own land.

He made cuttings, but kept them jealously for himself.

Which is how this variety came home again.

People have been fighting for it ever since . . .

The Copsolfruit cooperative, founded in 1961, produces 1,000 tons of the fruit (of which 95% is either the "boule d'or" or "violette" type), making the Var region the leading supplier for the domestic French market. **Locals move heaven and earth in defense of "their" figs, refer to the area as "the fig capital of the world," put up billboards, and organize an August Fig Festival.** This is when growers display their produce, a ceremonial fig tree is

planted, celebrity guests are invited to speak, official "friends of the fig" are appointed, a Fig Queen (known as "Fig Ambassadress") is elected, and meals featuring fig recipes are served . . .

Last year, 500 people attended the fig banquet. Although their numbers may have to be restricted somewhat this year, the ardent fig mania will no doubt remain undimmed. For the second time running, a "Fig Avenue" will be inaugurated with a parade of floats decorated by the festival committee.

These are people, in other words, who really love their figs—as if the fruit bound them to a more authentic past, one closer to the earth and to their roots.

✴ Harvest-time: from August 15th to November 15th for the "violette" variety, and from June 15th to July 15th for the "boule d'or," the variety native to Solliès-Pont.

Market day: ✴ Wednesdays, Place de l'Eglise ✴

The time, the place: if you want to savor your figs to the utmost after you've purchased them, wend your way to the fountain in the middle of the Place de l'Eglise and sample them at a table on one of the nearby café terraces.

The Fig Festival: held at the end of August. Includes exhibitions, inaugural ceremony, market stalls, local chapter of the *Confrérerie des Amis de la figue*, election of the Fig Ambassadress, children's games and (notably) on Saturday night at 9 P.M., a banquet featuring fig recipes.

Tourist Office: 04.94.28.92.35.

My recipe for figs au gratin with fennel

8 large figs, 5 tablespoons parmesan cheese, fresh bay leaf, pepper from the mill, 1 clove, 3 small fennel bulbs, rosemary, thyme, 1 3/4 cup Banyuls (local fortified wine), olive oil.

✴ Carefully wash the figs, pierce with a fork and place in the Banyuls with the sprigs of thyme and rosemary, laurel leaf, clove, and pepper (one turn of the mill). ✴ Allow to marinate for 3 hours at room temperature. ✴ Place the figs and marinade in a saucepan and simmer for 30 minutes over low flame. ✴ Wash the fennel bulbs, cut into quarters. Pour a little olive oil into a large frying pan and

lightly brown the fennel bulbs in the oil for about 10 minutes.

Preheat oven to 350° F.

* Arrange the figs evenly in a large ovenproof pan, add the quartered fennel bulbs, baste with 1/4 of the marinade. Bake for 20 minutes.

* Using a vegetable scraper, cut the parmesan cheese into thin strips and place on top of the figs. Bake for another 20 minutes and serve.

The ideal accompaniment: a mixture of ground veal, bacon, and herbs covered with leaves of spinach and baked in the oven for 45 minutes.

* * *

• The taste of Cavaillon melon

When summer rolls around, Jean-Jacques Prévôt's thoughts turn to melon. His restaurant is a vibrant hymn to this fruit. Napkin rings, ashtrays, water carafes, engravings on the wall, pottery, preserves, apéritifs, the menu —here's a place where "a cut of the melon" means just that, literally, since Prévôt isn't a gambling man. On the other hand, once you get him started, he's a jackpot of information on the subject, a lyric encyclopedia with chapters on each different variety (there exist over 25), the best types (luna star, lunabelle, mayol, charentais), the soil (the loamy soil on the banks of the Durance River), and, especially, the qualities he looks for: **"A juicy, sweet, crisp melon with firm flesh."**

He cannot understand the people who complain of insipid, disappointing melons. "It's like finding a good bakery. You don't buy your bread just anywhere, do you? Well, the same goes for melons. Shop around, be demanding. Then, like me for the past twenty years, you'll get exactly what you want!"

The best time of year? From July 14th to August 15th, but melons "hold their own" from April to October.

How do you recognize a good melon? It should be appealing to the eye, distinctly striped from end to end, bluish-green in color, evenly rounded. Its weight should be proportionate to its volume (big melons should be heavy, in other words).

How do you recognize a bad melon? Its skin is brownish-yellow, its shape is flattened rather than evenly rounded, it will be spotty.

How should you smell a melon? Tradition decrees that you should smell a melon at the blossom end (on the bottom, or tail), but real connoisseurs smell the top (or stem end), on the opposite pole of the blossom axis, since this is the portion that receives the most sunlight during growth.

What do people mean by "la tranche du roi?" Aha . . . This phrase refers to the so-called "royal" section on some melons, which is often free of seeds. When a growing melon is tilted in a certain way, the force of gravity pulls the seeds down into the blossom end as the stem end ripens under its extra share of sunlight.

Should you buy melons from roadside stands? Jean-Jacques Prévôt's answer is an unequivocal "No! That's where you find the melons growers were unable to get rid of elsewhere. Give them a wide berth."

The address: ✶Jean-Jacques Prévôt, 353 Avenue de Verdun, in Cavaillon (Vaucluse, 04.90.71.32.43)✶

The market: Cavaillon, two daily markets, Le Petit Marché and La Fruiterie.

The Melon Festival: in mid-July, at Cavaillon.

Melon country: if you want to wander the world of the melon, take a trip around Cucuron, the region with the best soil for cultivating melons.

• The taste of garlic

I know, I know. Garlic has a terrible reputation. It lingers on the breath, it overwhelms every dish to which it's added. This is so unfair! Because, without garlic, Provençal cuisine—Provence itself—would be unrecognizable. You might as well eliminate the local accent, drain the sea, muffle the locusts. The fact that you want to visit Provence implies that you accept the region's strength of character-and garlic is an integral part of it.

There are 250 species of garlic, but only 3 major types:

*White garlic, clad in a silvery white skin. This is the most common variety, grown primarily in Drome and especially Vaucluse.

* Rose garlic, its skin sometimes slightly veined with red, generally from Var.

* Red garlic, the skin of which is actually almost purple.

Remember: garlic season doesn't begin until May and ends in late summer.

Garlic naturally suggests aioli, one of the great recipes of Provence—made by pounding garlic in a mortar with olive oil and an egg yolk until a mayonnaise-like emulsion is formed. The greatest aioli specialists of the past, their eyes riveted on posterity, all had their own special recipes. For example, gastronomic prince Curnonsky used a boiled potato mashed with breadcrumbs soaked in milk, 2 sweet almonds, and 2 egg yolks to make his aioli.

Another favorite garlic dish is bourride, a fish stew served with aioli paste. Bouido, a Provençal soup, calls for thyme, bay leaf, and sage in addition to the garlic.

* Some "garlic hints:" to lessen garlic's "bad effects," boil it unpeeled for a few minutes; or, chew a few coffee beans, coriander seeds, or cloves after eating it. If you're planning to take a nap and don't want a snake to crawl into your mouth while you're sleeping (it could happen), just eat a clove of garlic before retiring and the snakes will stay away. Garlic is also thought to be an aphrodisiac, a bactericide, and a remedy for improving digestion and keeping melancholy at bay!

Garlic markets: numerous cities in the south of France honor garlic with special markets, such as the one held in Marseille from mid-June to mid-July on Cours Belsunce, and the Piolenc market (Avignon), held the last weekend in August.

My recipe for pistou

3 large garlic cloves, 2 bunches basil,
black pepper from the mill, "fleur de sel" salt, 2 tablespoons
freshly grated parmesan cheese, 1/2 cup extra-virgin olive oil

* Peel the garlic cloves and discard the inner green sprout. * Remove
leaves from basil stalks. * Place garlic and "fleur de sel" salt
in a mortar, and pound into a paste with the pestle. * Gradually add
the basil, crushing the leaves until a very smooth green paste is obtained.
* When all the basil has been reduced to a purée, add the olive oil
in a thin stream while continuing to pound with the pestle. Add the
grated parmesan and mix well. * Taste and adjust seasoning if necessary.
* Scrape into a bowl and serve immediately (on pasta, for example).

Pistou can be placed in a small jar and stored for several days
in the refrigerator. Coat the surface with a little olive oil. Pistou can
also be made in a blender, but the result will not be as good . . .

Ligurian pistou ("pesto") is a slight variation on the above recipe.
Pine nuts are added to the ingredients, and Pecorino (Italian
sheep's cheese) can be substituted for half of the parmesan .

* * *

• The taste of lamb

One of France's favorite meats "grows" in the Sisteron region. Here,
you're in the land of Jean Giono —the Alpes-de-Haute-Provence— with
its blue skies swept clean by the mistral, its cool hills carpeted in clover. Jean Suveran and his wife tend a flock of 300 ewes, 350 lambs,
and 4 rams on the plateau of Valensole. The animals roam
at will, grazing on alfalfa, wild clover, tarragon, hare's ear, dande-
lions, and thyme. They're an especially pretty sight under
the setting sun, clustering together and breaking apart, huddling in
small groups and then scattering.

Le Carré d'Agneau
avec sa garniture de
Civet
du Facteur
Rognons à la
Poussin à la
Fricassée
et aux
Haricots
sautés au
Salade

44

Meanwhile, Jean Suveran bides his time, savoring his utopia, his "luxury:" "My luxury is playing shepherd." His luxury is also to raise his lambs for 5 months, compared with the standard 3 months or so; to let the lambs mature naturally; and to linger —with us— in the cool of the evening until the animals finally decide to return to the fold. The results of all this attention are clearly visible on the plate: take a good look at the tenderness of the meat, savor its taste (of herbs, fresh air, local soil) and texture.

You're looking at what the region's restaurateurs call the "caviar" of Haute-Provence.

Unfortunately, the genuine article is incredibly difficult to find. The "Sisteron" label is too vague, "all too often applied to animals slaughtered in Sisteron, but not actually raised there," as Suveran explains. Genuine local lambs are not available throughout the year, but the demand for them continues to increase, year-long. The net is thus cast wider and wider, hauling in lambs from Aveyron, the Massif Central, the Loire region —and even Algeria. However, sensing a shift in consumer awareness, professionals have gone to work, launching what is known as "traceability." We're not out of the woods yet by any means, but the lamb-butchers of Sisteron do understand the urgency of the situation.

Where to find Sisteron lamb? All fine butcher shops in the region receive regular supplies, but be sure to explain that you want lamb raised in Sisteron—the butcher will understand at once.
Addresses: ✱Cannes (Alpes-Maritimes), Au Roi du Charolais, 38 Rue Meynadier (04.93.39.09.93)✱
✱Nice (Alpes-Maritimes), Agu, 20 Cours Saleya (04.93.62.32.74)✱
✱Fiorucci, 25 Route de Grenoble (04.93.83.11.17)✱

My recipe for oven-roasted milk-fed lamb, fennel dusted with parmesan, spring onions and fresh navy beans with savory

2 small legs of milk-fed lamb or 1 standard leg of lamb, 1 saddle of lamb plus the 2 racks, 1 neck of lamb (sliced), 4 milk-fed lamb kidneys studded with savory, 4 large firm fennel bulbs, 8 spring onions, 1 lb. fresh navy beans, 1 bunch savory, 4 cloves green garlic, 2 tablespoons grated parmesan, 2 tablespoons butter, olive oil, 1 cup chicken broth, Guérande salt, pepper from the mill, coarse salt.

* Preheat oven to 425° F * Rub all the meat with savory.
* Rinse the fennel and wipe dry, cut in half, flatten the rounded side, and cook until done in boiling salted water. * Shell the fresh beans, peel the spring onions and the green garlic. * In a large roasting pan, brown the lightly salted slices of lamb neck in the butter and olive oil. Add the rest of the meat and the kidneys (leaving most of the suet in place). Roast in a hot oven (425° F), baste, adding butter and olive oil if necessary. **Milk-fed lamb is served medium-rare.** *5 minutes before the meat is done (total roasting time about 20-30 minutes), add the spring onions and green garlic. * Remove meat from oven and place on a rack over a pan to drain. Remove green onions and green garlic to a side dish. Add a quarter of the chicken broth to roasting pan and scrape up particles attached to bottom of pan while simmering over a low flame, continuing to detach pan juices with a brush. Repeat this operation 3 times until all of the broth has been used. Strain into a saucepan. * Add the green onions, garlic, and a pinch of savory to the juices in saucepan, steep for a few moments and then add the juices drained from the cooked meat on the rack. * Heat to the simmering point and keep warm. * Brown the cooked fennel in a frying pan. When well browned, dust with parmesan and toss briefly. * Give the fresh navy beans a "turn" in the frying pan with the savory flower. * Arrange all ingredients on platter, cover with the warm pan-juice mixture, and serve.

* * *

• The taste of anchovies

These tiny fishes are social creatures that travel in schools. You'll never see an anchovy out for a solitary stroll. Or if you do, it means the little fellow has lost his way. Follow him, and he'll lead you to his silvery blue-green friends. The anchovy may be small and even insignificant, but it rates high on the popularity charts. Shifts in fashion periodically raise it from commonplace popularity to genuine esteem.

Anchovies are eaten fresh, salted, or fried. Despite its distinctive character, the anchovy is a docile little fish that lends itself to dishes of every kind. Wrapped in leaves of Swiss chard, in omelets, en papillote (cooked in foil or ovenproof paper), marinated in vinegar. Since the dawn of time, however, it has traditionally been particularly relished as the main ingredient in anchoïade, where it plays a starring role supported by olive oil, garlic, and pepper.

Anchoiade is a paste ideal for accompanying cooked or raw vegetables. Bear in mind, however, that the anchovy should reflect its simple origins, so don't move too far away from the classic, everyday recipes that respect its keen flavor. I'm thinking mainly of the dish known as pissaladière, which in my opinion is a model of its kind. It's a decidedly simple dish, homespun and generous. To me, a perfect reflection of Provence.

* Where to buy anchovies? Fishing ports (Martigues, Marseille) may seem the likeliest places to find anchovies, but the truth is that the best specimens are shipped immediately to restaurants, markets, etc.

• My recipe for marinated anchovies •

2 lbs. very fresh, good-sized anchovies, 2 cups white-wine vinegar, 1 quart extra-virgin olive oil, sea salt (fine), 3 tablespoons chopped flat parsley, 6 finely chopped cloves garlic.

*Remove heads from anchovies, clean and scale, rinse thoroughly, wipe dry, and extract the fillets (these operations can be done for you at your fish shop). * Place a layer of fillets in a large bowl, skin-side down. * Sprinkle the fillets with salt, cover with vinegar. * Repeat this process, in successive layers, until you have used all the anchovies. * Allow to marinate for 1 hour. * Drain the anchovies in a stainless-steel colander or strainer for 15 to 30 minutes. * Layer the drained fillets in a porcelain terrine, skin-side down. Sprinkle olive oil over each layer as you go. * Scatter the chopped garlic and parsley over the final layer, pour on the remaining oil. * Cover the terrine. * Allow to marinate for at least 12 hours before serving.

Marinated anchovies can be stored for up to 8 days in the refrigerator. After 3 days, they will be melting and delicious.

If desired, add slices of garlic, thin half-slices of (untreated) lemon, cloves, sweet peppers, and black peppercorns between the layers of anchovies in the terrine. Lastly, to prevent the olive oil from solidifying, you can replace 1/3 of it with an equal amount of grape-seed oil.

CHEESE

I always feel a twinge of regret when I see people skip the cheese course. They rush toward dessert and it's sugary delights, it's satiny magic. They're eager to set sail from salty climes and head for lands that are more clement, gentle, and beguiling.
And yet, the cheese course is a fundamental phase of the meal.
We've finished with prepared dishes, combinations of ingredients, the chemistry of sauces and complicated transformations. The time has come to savor a moment of peace and repose that's unadorned, natural.

The cheese course provides a moment of direct contact with a specific region, a countryside.

With the cheeses of Provence, I have the impression of being in direct touch with the region's fragrances and vegetation, its heat and the cool of its stones. The next time you sit down to a meal in Provence, spare a thought for this moment.

* * *

Provençal cheeses and where to find them

Apt (Vaucluse). ✳Fromagerie, 10 Rue de la Sous-Préfecture✳ A wide selection of goat and sheep cheeses.
You might want to sample the cheeses sold by ✳Elisabeth Murat (mild goat cheeses), at the market, opposite the Caisse d'Epargne (bank)✳ The products of the Maison Ricard are also worth a try.

Carpentras (Vaucluse). ✳La Fromagerie du Comtat, 23 Place Maurice Charretier (04.90.60.00.17)✳The Vigier family displays an intense passion for cheese, expressed through a very fine and extensive selection, and especially through the warm welcome that makes this address one of the best in the area.

Oppède (Vaucluse). ✳Geneviève Molinas, La Bastide de Fondos (04.90.72.26.71)✳ An interesting range of goat cheeses, plus a very fine Camembert.

Vaison-la-Romaine (Vaucluse). ✳Lou Canesteou, Josiane and Christian Deal, 10 Rue Raspail (04.90.36.31.30)✳ Excellent selection of goat cheeses; a choice of Patricia Wells, *International Herald Tribune* food critic.

Aix-en-Provence (Bouches-du-Rhône). ✳Gérard Paul, 9 Rue des Marseillais (04.42.23.16.84)✳ One of the best addresses in the city, run by a master cheese connoisseur who ages and markets the region's distinctive poetry, expanding it with additional verses from other parts of the country.

Noves (Bouches-du-Rhône). ✳Christian Fleury, 1960 Chemin de l'Eau (04.90.94.45.91)✳ Make an appointment at this farm specializing in goat cheeses, and stock up on *fleurons, gardians,* and *crottins des Alpilles.*

Banon (Alpes-de-Haute-Provence). ✳Fromagerie de Banon, Route de Carniol (04.92.73.25.03)✳ You'll find excellent Banon cheeses at Joël Corbon's (see below), but the selection here is also very fine.

Valensole (Alpes-de-Haute-Provence). ✳Simone and Charles Chabot, La Petite-Colle (04.92.74.81.92)✳ Official purveyors of cheese to the region's best restaurants, with special emphasis on the famed Banon, of course.

Cannes (Alpes-Maritimes). ✳Céneri, 22 Rue Meynadier (04.93.39.63.68)✳ The Céneris are expert agers and purveyors of cheese who offer a grand tour of the subject: regional varieties and a careful selection of parmesans, cheddars, and so on.

Nice (Alpes-Maritimes). ✳La Ferme fromagère, 27 Rue Lépante (04.93.62.52.34) and 3 Rue Maccarani (04.93.88.83.80)✳ One of the best addresses in Provence: a remarkable selection of cheeses from the region and elsewhere. Also a restaurant with a cheese-focused menu.

Moulinet (Alpes-Maritimes). Trannoy, 7 Rue de l'Eglise (04.93.04.81.88), and at the Cours Saleya market in Nice on Tuesdays, Saturdays, and Sundays.

✳ * ✳

The taste of real Banon cheese from Banon
(Banon is about 20 miles from Apt).

Banon cheese is like a continent, meandering over 38 cantons and pausing for breath at Drôme and Castellane as it crosses the Vaucluse and Lubéron mountains, the regions around Apt and Forcalquier, the Valensole plateau, Haut-Verdon, the Digne and Sisteron countryside. It comes to an end at the Jabron valley, in the Haute-Provence Alps.

For the past several years, local cheese-makers have been fighting to obtain the "appellation d'origine contrôlée" label, in order to stem the tide of inferior imitations proliferating at the fringes of their region.

For Banon is a highly prized cheese. Legend—which has a long life and an indiscriminate stomach—maintains that Roman emperor Anthony the Pious (86-161 A.D.) died of indigestion due to a surfeit of Banon. Well, maybe . . .

Banon is probably one of the most costly cheeses in the world: from 80 to 100F per pound ($10.70-13.50). When Banon trade-association president Joël Corbon alludes to this, he does so with almost apologetic diffidence. But the plain fact is, Banon doesn't exactly grow on trees. It's the fruit of a lengthy production process, the key to which is natural rather than lactic fermentation. Or, to put it simply: the process (based on pressure) is tricky and the yield small; the fermentation period painstaking; the risk great; and the cheese's life span short, since **a Banon cheese must be consumed within 8-15 days,** whereas the identical cheese produced by means of lactic fermentation has a life span of 6 months.

* How to recognize a genuine Banon cheese? It's biscuit-shaped, wrapped in a chestnut leaf, and tied with a strand of straw.
It always bears the label "Adhérent à la charte de Banon" and the following explanation: "**Banon from Haute-Provence is made from naturally fermented goat and/or sheep's milk, molded and aged in brown chestnut leaves.**"
Inferior imitations are wrapped in green leaves and, when unwrapped, the cheese inside is white, whereas genuine Banon inevitably displays traces of fermentation under its brown chestnut leaf.
The best season for enjoying Banon: in spring and autumn. Summer Banon has a lower fat content.

The address: *Joël Corbon, La Pourcine, Limans (04.92.73.01.54)*
The time, the place: at sunset, in the Gubian chestnut forest between the Banon and Forcalquier roads, near Revest-des-Brousses. Thrills guaranteed.
Contact: *Syndicat interprofessionnel de défense et de promotion du Banon* (trade association), Maison Régionale de l'Elevage, Route de la Durance, Manosque (Alpes-de-Haute-Provence, 04.92.87.47.55).
Training programs: during the off-season, you can learn how Banon is made by calling Joël Corbon, at La Pourcine, in Limans (04.92.73.01.54).
www.emery-info.fr/banon: for the history of Banon and how it's produced.
The book: *Fromages fermiers en Provence et dans les Alpes du Sud,* Editions Barthélemy.

BREAD, CAKES, AND PASTRY

French cuisine may be on the move—flying off in all directions, swinging, almost vanishing under a profusion of new dishes—but I sense that the world of bread and cake remains above the fray, maintaining a kind of dignity in response to all this agitation, as if bread and cake were guardians of the temple, the protectors of tradition and continuity.

The connecting link for any meal—now as in the past—is bread, whether French baguette, flat or round country loaf, etc.

Bread gives me a sense of being sustained, as by the banister beside a flight of stairs. It represents constancy, fidelity, recollected time, the conscience of gastronomy. When I cook, when a great new idea occurs to me, there's always a piece of bread (or a peppercorn, a grain of rice . . .) to remind me that it's important to keep things simple. Bread is my guardian angel, my secret garden.

Cakes are more fickle, despite their expansiveness. They are alert to fashion and sometimes mimic it, but they have about them a desire to please, give pleasure, do their best, that gives them a touch of humanity—superficial yet substantial. Thus, when I cross the threshold of a bakery or pastry shop, I feel as though I'm stepping into the pages of a book recounting the story of my own time, my era. This is why I invite you, too—if only for the pleasure of eye and nose—to step into a good bakery-pastry-shop and contemplate the loving work performed by its master craftsmen as they turn out **bread, panisses, fougasses, and pissaladières. You'll see what I mean. These things really speak to you!**

• • •

✻ Where to find bread, cakes, and pastry ✻

Mérindol (Vaucluse). ✻Le Fournil de Mérindol, 12 Rue du Relarguier (04.90.72.96.04)✻ *Fougasses.* Speed is not of the essence when it comes to making *fougasse.* Take your time, let the idea develop, choose your olives, your olive oil (here it carries the "organic" label), your flour (it's from the Haute-Provence Alpes, carries the "organic" label, and is therefore twice as expensive), your leavening (none of this chemical stuff). In this instance, slow and steady equals very good. Here, the worktable is magnificent in its plain chestnut-wood austerity, the fire is made from poplar, the oven built of Biot stone. The kneading machine doesn't spin like a top, but turns slowly, so the dough won't oxidize or overheat and turn acid. There are no stainless-steel or plastic utensils—both bake room and shop appear to have survived from an earlier time. If you want to savor your fougasse to the utmost, tuck it under your arm and stroll down the Route de l'Observatoire to the banks of the Durance, find a shady spot on the pebbly bank, sit back and enjoy it at leisure. When to buy it? Some people like it hot out of the oven, and if you're one of them, bear in mind that batches of fresh *fougasse* are baked on Mondays, Wednesdays, and Fridays in the late afternoon. Stop by around 7 P.M. A *fougasse* weighing one pound costs 25 F ($3.50).

Velleron (Vaucluse). ✻Franck Bouvier, Place Jean Jaurès (04.90.20.01.47)✻ One of the best bakers in the area, a man who works according to the ancestral rules.

Maillane (Bouches-du-Rhône). ✻Boulangerie Fassy, 4 Cours Jeanne-d'Arc (04.90.95.74.01, closed from end of June through mid-July)✻ Monsieur Fassy and his son run a bakery-bookshop displaying every possible variation on the *fougasse.*

Marseille (Bouches-du-Rhône). ✻A l'Estaque, Papa Rozzonnelli's stall in front of the bakery, Place de l'Estaque✻ For his *panisses* (see p. 60, "The taste of *panisse*").

✻Boulangerie Michel Séverin, 33 Rue Vacon (04.91.33.79.43)✻ If you're looking for the famous leavened bread of Marseille, you've come to the right door.

Saint-Rémy-de-Provence (Bouches-du-Rhône). ✻Le Petit Duc, run by Anne Daguin and Frédérik Gaudichon, 7 Boulevard Victor Hugo (04.90.92.08.31)✻ A charming gourmet shop where genuine research and creativity rule: *pastilles d'amour, pignolats* inspired by Nostradamus's treatise on jams, *calissons* and other treats.

Le Tholonet (Bouches-du-Rhône). Boulangerie L'Epi d'or, Avenue Paul Julien Palette (04.42.66.95.06)✻ A treasure-trove of a bakery with a wide selection of different breads.

Moustiers-Sainte-Marie (Alpes-de-Haute-Provence). ✻Boulangerie Les Michons, Robert Pelx, Place Couvert (04.92.74.66.31)✻ All types of bread, naturally—whole-grain, leavened, traditional—and also a *fougasse* with orange flower and this baker's famous *michon.*

Antibes (Alpes-Maritimes). ✻Boulangerie-pâtisserie Jean Carlevan, 8 Rue Sade (04.93.34.78.46)✻ Here, bathed in a waft of fragrance from the oven, you'll find the famous Antibes *michettes*, plus a wide and varied selection of other breads.

Gattières (Alpes-Maritimes). ✻At two shops run by Maguy and Laurent Campana, one on Rue du 8 Mai, the other at 17 Rue Pontis (04.93.08.63.12)✻ It's a rare treat to see so many varieties of bread (at least fifty!), reflecting a fertile love of the subject. Varieties made with anchovies, whole grain or spelt flour, natural leavening, olive oil, and much more.

Nice (Alpes-Maritimes). ✻Thérésa, 28 Rue Droite (04.93.85.00.04, closed Mondays)✻ Also at a Cours Saleya stall on market days. Fabulous *soccas.*

Vieil-Antibes (Alpes-Maritimes). ✻Jean-Paul Veziano, 2 Rue de la Pompe (04.93.34.05.46.)✻ For its savory *pissaladières.*

The taste of panisse

Panisse is symbolic of good cheer and a peasant culture.
The origin of this fritter made from chickpea meal goes back quite a way. The people of Marseille probably developed their abiding taste for chickpeas in the sixteenth century, when the king's navy was blockading the port. Legend has it that, one fine Palm-Sunday morning, the populace awoke to the sight of a Spanish galleon lying in port, its hold filled with chickpeas. Thus saved from imminent famine, Marseille has ever afterward maintained a loving relationship with chickpeas in every guise. One of these is panisse, a small golden disk with strong sentimental associations, even though current fashion has yet to catch up with it.

If a friend from Marseille invites you to the port of l'Estaque to sample a few panisses, it's important to realize he's actually offering you the keys to his city.

Despite the noise and fumes of traffic, the seafront's three purveyors of panisse are still holding out.
"Papa" Rozzonnelli weaves a web of mystery around his recipe for panisse, a secret he had to drive a hard bargain for in 1986, when he purchased his small business. The former owner agreed to relinquish the recipe only at the last possible moment, and only in the presence of a lawyer. Today Rozzonnelli's stall attracts crowds from all walks of life.

Where to find "Papa" Rozzonnelli? ✴ At L'Estaque, in front of the bakery on the Place de l'Estaque✴ His daughter Magali works with him; his son Thierry officiates in the other bakery, opposite the nearby pharmacy.
His secret: water, chickpea meal, salt, very fresh oil for frying, and that's it!
His advice: for extra zest, sprinkle a little pepper on your *panisse* before eating—it makes all the difference!
Where to buy *panisses*? From almost any shop selling freshly-made pasta, and specifically: in Nice, at ✴ Barale (Rue Sainte-Réparate), Tosello (on the same street), at Raviolis Perrin, in Antibes (Cours Masséna), and in Grasse, at Azur Pâte (Avenue Pierre Semard)✴
A time, a place: when you've purchased your paper cone of *panisses* (12 F – $1.60), sit down on a nearby bench to enjoy its contents at leisure, or savor them with a glass of rosé wine on a café terrace.
The best time of day? On your way home from the beach.

My recipe for panisse

1 to 1 1/2 cups chickpea meal to 1 quart water. Olive oil, salt, pepper.

* Add a few tablespoons of olive oil to the water and bring to a boil.
* When the water is boiling, add the chickpea meal in a steady stream, stirring briskly until smooth. Cook for approximately 10 minutes.
* Before the mixture has time to cool and harden, mold it into the desired shape. Use tall cylindrical molds (for round panisses) or shallow pans (for sticks) that have been moistened with water or spread with a little oil. The mixture can also be molded by rolling it up in a clean dish towel to form a long tubular shape—the method preferred in Marseille. Molding is the hardest part of the operation.
* Allow the molded dough to rest undisturbed for 2 hours. * Slice the molded panisse dough into rounds (using the tubular or cylindrical shapes) or sticks (using the flat shapes) measuring just under an inch in thickness. * Fry in hot olive oil until golden-brown.

Panisses can be served with a sauce, as a side dish; or with sugar, as a dessert (in this case, omit the pepper).

They can also be served au gratin, sprinkled with cheese and baked until crisp and golden in the oven. Panisses aren't costly, but they can be tricky to make successfully.

* * *

The Thirteen Desserts

Although of course not everyone observes it to the letter, Provençal Christmas tradition specifies the use of three white tablecloths, "**one for the Father, one for the Son, and one for the Holy Ghost**", or, in practice, one for the big Christmas dinner on the night of the 24th, one for lunch on the 25th, and one for lunch on the 26th. One of the cloths is removed after each meal, but the setting remains the same throughout the three days. The menu, whether at home or in a restaurant, can include almost anything—foie gras, lobster—although the classic Provençal Christmas dinner is lean. There is one tradition everybody still enjoys, however, and that's the Christmas cake known as "**gibassier**" (because it has humps; "gibou" in the local dialect means "hunchback").

Giving the thirteen desserts a try:

Each canton has its own version of the thirteen desserts, but all of Provence is represented in the following list. First comes the gibassier (or pompe à l'huile) that, when broken, ensures prosperity throughout the New Year. Then comes black nougat and white nougat (the "Capucine" variety, with figs, walnuts, and honey). Followed by mendiants (or mendicants, a "mendicant-monk" medley including dried gray figs, like the gray habit of Franciscan monks; dark raisins, like the dark habit of the Augustans; light-brown almonds, like the light-brown habit of the Dominicans and barefoot Carmelites). Then fresh fruit (apples, pears, oranges, tangerines), dried fruit (dates), sweets (calissons d'Aix or casse-dents d'Allauch), fritters, au gratin desserts, and pastries. After doing justice to all of this, we might—should the spirit move us—try to make amends for anything weighing on our conscience by paying the customary end-of-year visits of reconciliation.

The recipe for gibassier

2 lbs. (about 4 cups) basic bread dough,
4 cups additional flour, 2 cups sugar, 1 1/2 cups olive oil

* Dissolve the sugar in a little water. * Add the oil.
* Blend this mixture with the basic bread dough and add additional flour until the dough can be formed into a smooth, firm ball.
* Allow to rise for about 1 hour. * Preheat oven to 450° F *
Break off pieces of the dough and roll them into small balls.
Place the balls on an oiled cookie sheet and bake for
12 to 15 minutes * For extra flavor, add orange zest
to the dough.

The taste of spelt

The latest craze in Provence is spelt, a primitive grain that was widespread in the distant past but has since languished in oblivion. Most cookbooks don't even mention its existence, thus turning a blind eye on ten thousand years of history.

Today, however, some chefs have rediscovered this "covered" grain (all of its nutritive value resides in the skin covering the kernel) so unlike "uncovered" varieties (such as the easier-to-handle wheat), and are using it as a powerful and versatile ally for adding a distinctive note to desserts as well as bread. North of Apt (Vaucluse), around the ravishing village of Sault, **this caviar of grains** has found the ideal soil-rough, clayey (olive-grove soil) for supporting its renaissance.

• • •

Make your own spelt bread with Edouard Loubet

Moulin de Lourmarin chef Edouard Loubet uses: 4 cups white flour, 6 cups spelt flour, 2 cups cooked cracked spelt, 12 tablespoons yeast, 4 tablespoons salt, 10 cups water

*Blend all ingredients and knead the dough (with beater, mechanical kneader, or by hand) thoroughly. * Using the hands, break pieces off dough and shape into small balls. * Place the balls of dough on a greased or oiled cookie sheet. Cover with a clean cloth and allow to rise at room temperature until double in bulk. Or, omit the cloth and spray the balls with water at regular intervals to prevent formation of a crust. * Preheat oven to 450° F.

* Bake until done (15 minutes or more, depending on size of balls).

The address: ✳Le Moulin de Lourmarin, Rue du Temple, Lourmarin (Vaucluse, 04.90.68.06.69)✳

A few restaurants famous for dishes containing spelt

Cavaillon (Vaucluse). ✳Le Prévot, 353 Avenue de Verdun (04.90.71.32.43)✳ A worthy defender of spelt (and melons . . .). From 130 to 470 F ($17–63).

Gordes (Vaucluse). ✳Elisabeth Bourgeois, Le Mas Tourteron, Route des Imberts (04.90.72.00.16)✳ Spelt polenta with spicy caramelized young hare, spelt *taboulé* with olive oil, spelt risotto with fresh baby vegetables. From 170 to 310 F ($23–41).

Lourmarin (Vaucluse). ✳Reine Sammut, in her brand-new Fenière, Route de Cadenet (04.90.68.11.79)✳, offers spelt gnocchi with a ragout of dried beans, artichoke hearts, and country bacon. From 200 to 550 F ($27–73).

✳Le Moulin de Lourmarin, Rue du Temple (04.90.68.06.69)✳ Edouard Loubet's novel contribution is an old-fashioned spelt basket containing ice cream made from Lourmarin-almond-milk served with aged plum brandy. On the salt side of the menu, truffle soup in season and (currently) a *bouriole*, or fried bread, with steamed fillet of cod and heart of sunflower. From 200 to 660 F ($27–88).

Reine Sammut's spelt gnocchi

Serves six. ✳ Preheat oven to 375° F. ✳ Wash 1 pound unpeeled potatoes, wipe dry, place in ovenproof pan and bake for 30 minutes, or until tender. ✳ Peel potatoes and mash or put through ricer to obtain a smooth purée. ✳ To the mashed potatoes, add 3 tablespoons spelt flour, 1 whole egg, 2 egg yolks, 1 tablespoon olive oil, salt, and white pepper from the mill. ✳ Sprinkle flour onto a flat surface and shape the gnocchi dough into small cylinders. Cut the cylinders of dough into slices just under 1 inch thick. ✳ Score the sides of each gnocchi with the back of a fork. ✳ Drop the gnocchi into a large pot of boiling water. ✳ The gnocchi will sink to the bottom of the pot and rise again to the surface when cooked. Remove the cooked gnocchi with a skimmer and drain on absorbent paper.

Reine Sammut serves her gnocchi with baked turbot and truffled beurre-blanc sauce.

The address: ✳Reine Sammut, La Fenière, Route de Cadenet, Lourmarin (Vaucluse, 04.90.68.11.79)✳

Where to find spelt? At the Coopérative de Sault (23 miles north of Apt), untreated spelt flour—sifted, unsifted, or blended with other grains.

To read: *Le Livre de l'épeautre*, Edisud.

My recipe for potato gnocchi

2 pounds starchy potatoes (Idaho),
1 1/2 cups flour, 1 egg,
2 tablespoons olive oil,
nutmeg, sea salt (fine).

*Wash potatoes, place in pot, cover with cold water, and boil over high flame until tender. * Drain and peel the cooked potatoes, put through a ricer (small holes). *To the riced potatoes, add the olive oil, 1 cup of the flour, the nutmeg (ground), egg, and salt. * Using the fingertips, blend the ingredients rapidly until a smooth ball is formed. * Sprinkle a pastry marble (or smooth countertop) with the remaining flour, and roll pieces of the potato mixture into cylinders approximately 1/3 inch in diameter. Cut the tubes into slices about half inch thick. You can score them with a fork to give them the typical "gnocchi" appearance, but this requires a certain knack . . . Bring a large pot of salted water to a rolling boil and drop in the gnocchi, which will sink to the bottom of the pot. The gnocchi are done when they rise to the surface again. * Remove from pot with a skimmer and drain on absorbent paper.

Gnocchi can be served in a variety of ways: with tomato or mushroom sauce, au gratin with parmesan cheese, or plain with a little butter.

* * *

WINE

A convivial wine, in any case,
one that charms you like a faithful
dog begging for affection.

I don't know why, but I place wine in a realm apart. Whereas cuisine provides an immediate, fleeting, instantaneous sensation, the world of wine is one of lingering pleasure. Of longevity, in fact. When I sip a wine, I have the impression of being projected into an entirely different order of things. My glass may contain five, ten, or sometimes even thirty years of patient waiting for a single instant—the instant the wine touches my lips. Wine is both completely abstract and yet symbolically expressive of a tangible reality reflected by soil, grapes, rootstock, and the shadow-world inside the cask. It is also the projection of a land, a region. When it comes to the wines of Provence, specifically, I don't seek technical prowess or competition with Bordeaux and Burgundies. Not at all. I just want to close my eyes, inhale its aromas, and recreate in my own way the land it was grown in. I want to recognize the exact hillside and texture of the earth—even the cap worn by the vintner as he makes his rounds. I want to visualize the blue of the sky, the breezes rippling over the sea, the triple mirror-play of sunlight on water, stone, and its own golden beams.

A wine of Provence affords simple pleasure, to be enjoyed at siesta time or while strolling through a shady arbor. A convivial wine, in any case, one that charms you like a faithful dog begging for a little affection.

Where to find the wines of Provence

Cairanne (Vaucluse). ✳Marcel Richaud, Route de Rasteau (04.90.30.85.25)✳ Fruity, spicy Côtes-du-Rhône wines (30 F – $4), and also local Cairanne wines that are bold and concentrated (yield: 1,000 liters per acre), made from old Grenache, Syrah, and Mourvèdre rootstock (65 F – $8.70).

Pertuis (Vaucluse). ✳Château Val Joanis, Chemin Val de Joanis (04.90.79.20.77)✳ Côtes-de-Lubéron. A spectacular site with an excellent cellar on a 445-acre estate restored in the 1970s by the Chancel family.

Saint-Rémy-de-Provence (Bouches-du-Rhône). ✳Château Romanin, Les Baux-de-Provence (04.90.92.45.87)✳ Over 600 acres, including 125 acres planted in organically tended vineyards, backed up by incredible cellars combining neo-Gothic and neo-Egyptian architecture. This is definitely the most theatrical tourist stop in Provence.

Palette (Bouches-du-Rhône). ✳Château Simone, 13590 Leyreuil (04.42.66.92.58)✳ One of the smallest French estates (75 acres), half of which belongs to the Rougier family—owners of the château depicted on one of the most appealing labels in the trade. Excellent wines, among the finest in Provence.

Les Arcs-sur-Argens (Var). ✳Maison des Vins des Côtes-de-Provence, N 7 (04.94.99.50.20)✳ Includes a shop selling regional products and books on wine, plus Le Bacchus Gourmand restaurant. A satisfying stop for hungry and thirsty connoisseurs.

Bandol (Var). ✳Château de Pibarnon, La Cadière-d'Azur (04.94.90.12.73)✳ Great Bandol wines with a full-bodied bouquet (notes of leather, fig, and tobacco). Estate with a charming hillside location.
✳Château Pradeaux, 83270 Saint-Cyr-sur-Mer (04.94.32.10.21)✳ A truly authentic Bandol (95% Mourvèdre compared with only 50% usually found under other Bandol labels). A fine wine made according to traditional methods.

Cabasse (Var). ✳Domaines Gavoty (04.94.69.72.39)✳ On this estate the Gavoty family produces some of the best Côtes-de-Provence wines, including a fine Claredon vintage featuring an intensely fruity Syrah grape. Expect a warm welcome.

✳   ✳

A few AOC wines:
(official "Appellation d'Origine Contrôlée" labeled)
AOC Bandol: Domaine Sorin, Saint-Cyr-sur-Mer (Var, 04.92.92.86.43).

AOC Côtes-de-Provence: Domaine Rabiega, Clos d'Ière, Saint-Cyr-sur-Mer (Var, 04.94.68.44.22).

AOC Côtes-de-Provence: Domaine Richeaume, Puyloubier (Bouches-du-Rhône, 04.42.66.31.27).

AOC Coteaux varois: Château La Curnière, Tavernes (Var, 04.94.72.39.31).

Provence – almost too good to be true

Provence's biggest problem is also its major asset: an infinite variety that defies description. Provence is one of those darlings of nature that doesn't have to make any effort to be noticed—it gets plenty of notice just by existing. When you study a wine map of Provence, for example, you suddenly realize your eyes are wandering. Beguiled by a host of evocative place names (Vence, Manosque, Saint-Rémy, Le Lavandou) and arrested by cities of legendary fame (Marseille, Toulon, Cannes, Nice), you soon forget what you were looking for in the first place.

But let's get down to brass tacks and try to keep our minds on the job. Note, first of all, that there are nine official "appellations" in the region. They fall under the following geographical listings: Coteaux d'Aix, Coteaux des Baux, Côtes du Lubéron, Coteaux Varois. Within this first group, between the end of Côtes-du-Rhône and the beginning of Côtes-de-Provence, the standardization of recent years and an overall improvement in wine quality have blurred individual distinctions.

You have to have an exceptionally keen palate to identify the distinctive characteristics of a vintage, given that personalities (or the total absence of thereof) of the estate-owners have tended to overwhelm the authenticity of each respective region.

For the **Côtes-de-Provence appellation**, on the other hand, the complexity of the respective wines more or less faithfully reflects the diversity of the soils in which the grapes are grown. Here, on 44,500 acres located between Aix-en-Provence and Nice, we have an example of an area exhibiting genuine variety. First comes the zone around the Mont-Saint-Victoire massif with its clayey sandstone; then the chalky Beausset basin and the interior valley (sandy clay); ending with the Mediterranean coastline and the Maures massif with its shale and granite.

Paul Roux (left) at "Robinson"

Cellars at Château Romanin,
an incredible setting combining
neo-Gothic and neo-Egyptian styles.
Definitely the most theatrical site
in Provence . . .

By happy accident, most Côtes-de-Provence vineyards boast a permeable, pebbly soil poor in humus and benefit from the region's low rate of rainfall (24 inches concentrated in the spring and autumn). These conditions stimulate the growth of sturdy, aggressive vines that penetrate deep beneath the soil, where they find water and acquire their characteristic bouquet. When you add to this mix a violent, unrelenting mistral (perfect for keeping the vines healthy), a wide variety of rootstocks (13 in all), and exceptional luminosity, you're bound to obtain wine in all three colors (red, white, rosé) with a strong impact.

Take **Palette**, for example, grown in an area about as big as a pocket handkerchief. The makers of two-way radios would go out of business if all vineyards were on this Lilliputian scale (50 acres).

Two vintners and products of rare quality give some idea of the heights to which Provence wines can rise. The same impression is projected by the **Cassis** *appellation*, under which we find particularly pleasant, subtly aromatic whites.

However, it's with Bandol wines that Provence really shows off. There it is —lively, powerful, focused— appearing to have drawn from the historical past a degree of elegance and nobility artfully combined through the wine's spicy and peppery notes with a keen sense of the present. Certain labels for Bandol wines are real attention-getters as well, some featuring archaic calligraphy and others patrician crenelated châteaux. The list of Provence wines draws to a discreet close with the **extremely interesting white wines of Bellet.** And then, the final notes of this symphony fade, back go trumpets and violas into their cases, the piano under its dust cover.

Provence often finds itself the victim of its own charm. The region's rosé wines have locked it into the image of a beguiling idiot (or simpleton, if you prefer). People expect its wines to be "fun," to stay put in their leafy arbors, to be cheerful and amusing. That's the general idea, that's what people like . . . . Meanwhile, however, and here we see the region's underlying strength, heroic efforts on the part of maverick vintners throughout the area are beginning to bear fruit, exploding the insipid cliché of cheerful, "easy-drinking" wines and restoring the original nobility to vintages that as long ago as 600 B.C. were already enchanting the Phoenicians, including a certain Protis, to whom the king's daughter Gyptis offered a goblet of Provence wine symbolizing her love for him.

The taste of liqueur wines

Surely there's an explicit link, like an open book, between a product and the person who produces it. Take Jean Salen and his daughter Carole, for example. When you hold a bottle of their liqueur wine in your hands — before you've even opened it — you grasp the sum of their spiritual generosity. The wine itself is mild, subtle, appealing. It's a smash hit at dessert time, and I've more than once witnessed the birth of an unshakable passion for it after just a few sips. Here we have a totally unpretentious wine, the reflection of an inherent character.

Jean and Carole Salen's method is simple: they carefully nurture and cultivate their vineyards (Grenache rootstock) and harvest only perfectly ripe grapes.

The next step is even simpler. After pressing, the grape juice is simmered for 6 hours over an open fire. The lengthy fermentation period lasts for approximately one month. The wine is then filtered, just in time for the end-of-year holidays.

Jean Salen first decided to embark on the renewal of liqueur wine production in 1976, at a period when this type of wine was going through a particularly bad patch, the victim of too many misadventures and dubious interpretations. Ever since, the Les Bastides liqueur wine has ranked as one of the best of its kind. It is served by the finest

restaurants, and its limited annual production of 5,000 to 6,000 bottles (40% for the export market) makes it much sought after. It also offers connoisseurs the unaccustomed treat of seeing wine merchants show actual regret at having to part with a few of the precious bottles. On the basis of this success, liqueur wine is currently undergoing a strong revival. Take advantage of the few seasons of grace left to us for enjoying it whenever we want. Soon it will have become a truly rare wine.

* **How to recognize a bad liqueur wine?** Easy. It will be cloying to the taste and too dark to the eye (a blackish color indicates the addition of caramel).

* **Is there an official "appellation" in this category?** Alas, no.
As a result we encounter many dubious versions of this type, something that is not true of must-wines (like Rastau) which have their fermentation arrested by the addition of alcohol.

* **What to drink with it?** It can be enjoyed on its own, of course, but is also a superb accompaniment for desserts, with a special affinity for almonds, apricots, and pears. It is also not bad at all with spicy dishes, chocolate, even foie gras. A claim is also made for the happy marriage between liqueur wine and pork roasted with pineapple (perhaps!).

***A time, a place:** if you're seeking an appropriate spot in which to enjoy a glass of liqueur wine while contemplating the land it's grown in, you won't have to look far. Go to the hill of Quileo, where the village of Le Puy-Sainte-Réparade once stood before it was wiped off the map by an earthquake (in 1909). The new village stands today at the foot of the hill.

The address: * Domaine Les Bastides, owned by Carole and Jean Salen, Route de Saint Canadet, 13610 Le Puy-Sainte-Réparade (Bouches-du-Rhône, 04.42 61.97.66) * Open daily from 9 A.M. to noon and from 2 P.M. to 6:30 P.M. A bottle of liqueur wine costs between 80 and 125 F ($11-17). Also available in Paris from Les Caves Augé (8th Arrond.), Les Caves de l'Os à Mœlle (15th Arrond.), and Les Caves Daumesnil (12th Arrond.).

Ma thèse tient.
— C'est que vous la soutenez

La Vérité existe on n' invente que le mensonge.

HONEY

*If Provence sometimes wearies you with its "over-intensity,"
its endless pilgrimages, its tyranny of the exquisite,
you should head north . . .*

. . . . Which isn't too complicated, after all. In fact, it's a major tourist classic. Move away from the beaten path and head for the **Plateau de Valensole.** Suddenly the sky clears, silence reigns, breezes caress the landscape, the heavens rejoice —this is the real Provence.

In summertime, the lavender is in full bloom.

It gives a superb rhythm to the landscape, redesigns the geography, wafts its fragrance over the land and into our lungs. But . . . where is everybody? The plateau appears deserted. Except for a few bees. From mid-June through July, bees are gathered to produce their honey from this superb lavender, since **lavender thrives particularly well here.** Why? Because the plateau is extremely dry, producing a flower that is purer, denser, more colorful. The other side of the coin is that this particularly dry region sometimes suffers from drought.

This is good for the lavender, but not so good for the bees.

The drought conditions prevailing over the past three or four years have had beekeepers praying for rain during honey season as fervently as for the coming of the Messiah.

They're still waiting. These years are referred to as "catastrophic," and that's an understatement. Bees can only gather pollen from open blossoms, and it takes rain to open them.

So, next time you complain about rain spoiling your holiday in Provence, spare a thought for the beekeepers, and one of the best honeys in the region. In this land of miracles,

honey needs a shower of rain . . .

82

Where to find the honey of Provence . . .

Bonnieux (Vaucluse). ✱ Le Mas des Abeilles, Col Le Pointu (04.90.74.29.55, mas-des-abeilles.com) ✱ Superbly located on the Apt road (D943) at Lourmarin, 3 miles from Bonnieux. Here's a honey you won't find in any market—but only here. All the traditional varieties—rosemary, lavender, thyme—plus honey vinegar and honey-based confectionery.

Caumont-sur-Durance (Vaucluse). ✱ Renée and Jean-Marie Laurenti, 1 Traverse des Bourgades (04.90.23.00.71) ✱ This retired couple regularly wins awards in competition for honey made from lavender, rosemary (no production in 2000), acacia, and heather. Also available at the Le Pontet (near Avignon) market, open Thursdays.

Sault (Vaucluse). ✱ Jean Cartoux, Avenue de l'Oratoire (04.90.64.02.32) ✱ The Sault plateau is famous for its honey, and you're sure to find first-class varieties at this producer's (note his unusual "forest" honey).

Beaurecueil (Bouches-du-Rhône). At the foot of the Roussettes hill, among the rock rose and green oak, Jennifer Rocchia produces honey "the old-fashioned way," slowly, without frills. Wonderful flavors. ✱ You'll find her on D58, just off the crossroads between Beaurecueil and Pont-de-Bayeux ✱

Coudoux (Bouches-du-Rhône). ✱ François Bertin, 6 Avenue Alphonse Daudet (04.42.52.00.80) ✱ Definitely one of the best honeys in the region, including a remarkable "mountain" version.

Ampus (Var). ✱ Didier Gouillet, Hameau Lentier (04.94.67.03.14) ✱ On-site production of honeys based on lavender, heather, and rosemary. Also of interest: the Draguignan market (Saturday mornings).

Cotignac (Var). ✱ Les Ruchers du Bessilon, 2 Rue Naïs (04.94.04.60.39) ✱ 800 hives throughout Provence supply the honey (acacia, lavender, multifloral, etc.) sold by Fabienne and Laurence Guieu. www.séjour-en-provence.com/ruche 02.htm.

Vidauban (Var). ✱ Exploitation du Rey d'Agneou, Quartier Rey d'Agneou (04.94.73.56.37) ✱ At Jean-Claude Daval's apiary you'll find an extensive variety of honeys—chestnut, lavender, pine, lime-blossom—plus dandelion and oak. Daval also maintains stalls at regional markets, notably Mouans-Sartoux (Thursdays).

Barcelonnette (Alpes-de-Haute-Provence). ✱ Honey from the hives of Barcelonnette, La Valette, Saint-Pons (04.92.81.07.89) ✱ Jean-Charles Rampini works successfully with all types: lavender, acacia, multifloral, and a delicious chestnut.

Moustiers-Sainte-Marie (Alpes-de-Haute-Provence). Two good addresses: ✱ Raymond Courbon, Place de la Fondue (04.92.74.66.14) ✱ featuring renowned honeys, especially lavender; and then, of course, ✱ Marcel Scipion, Quartier Saint Jean (04.92.74.67.36) ✱, assisted by his son, marketing products that are especially fine.

Riez (Alpes-de-Haute-Provence). ✱ Patrice Zorzan, Rue du Marché (04.92.77.88.29, daily from 9:30 A.M. to 12:30 P.M. and from 3 P.M. to 7 P.M.) ✱ Zorzan sells honey produced by his cousins (25F a pound – $3.40). A choice of four types including rosemary (a recent addition). Royal jelly also available (270 F per ounce – $36).

Grasse (Alpes-Maritimes). ✱ Olivier Maure, Le Rucher de Maule, 123 Route de Draguignan (04.93.77.80.54) ✱ For his bitter arbutus honey.

Le Tignet (Alpes-Maritimes). ✱ Jean-Louis Lautard, 343 Avenue du Docteur Beletrud (04.93.66.12.15) ✱ Award-winning honeys, of course, and a well-deserved renown for one of the pioneers of honey who predictably offers delectable varieties—heather, multifloral, acacia, pine, chestnut.

My favorite recipe for "magaloumet" nougat

2 cups very fresh natural almond paste (or 1 3/4 cups finely
ground almonds, 1 tablespoon almond oil, 1 cup confectioner's sugar),
2 cups honey, 1 cup chopped almonds, 14oz. dark chocolate,
1 tablespoon heavy cream.

* If no natural almond paste is available, you can make your own: place the ground almonds, almond oil, and 1 cup confectioner's sugar in a bowl. Stir until blended, then knead until a smooth paste is obtained. Use some confectioner's sugar to dust the hands, fingertips, and a pastry board. Shape the almond paste (either prepurchased natural paste or what you have just made yourself) into small, finger-sized rolls. * Cut the rolls into slices about 1-inch thick and lay them one-by-one on the pastry board. * Being careful not to flatten the slices, place the uncovered board in a cool place (or the refrigerator) and allow to dry for 2 hours. * Pour the honey into a small frying pan and bring to a boil. When the honey begins to darken in color, add the chopped almonds. * Stir continuously and rapidly with a wooden spoon until all the almond pieces are thoroughly coated and the mixture is well blended. * When the mixture turns light caramel in color, remove immediately from flame. Oil one or more cake racks. * Spear the slices of chilled almond paste with small skewers and dip into the caramel mixture, rotating until each slice is completely coated. Work swiftly to prevent the slices of almond paste from melting or cooking. * Place the slices of caramel-coated almond paste on a cake rack to dry.

* If the caramel mixture becomes too stiff, reheat briefly, stirring continuously. When the mixture again comes to a boil, remove immediately from the flame and continue dipping.

* Allow the caramel-coated slices of almond paste to cool slightly.

* Melt the chocolate over a low flame or in a double-boiler, add the cream and blend. Remove the caramel-coated slices of almond paste from the rack (if some of the slices stick to the rack, detach gently with a thin knife), and dip into the chocolate-and-cream mixture. Return to cake rack and allow to cool thoroughly. Remove from rack and store.

Recipe from "Douceurs de Provence,"
by Maguelonne Toussaint-Samat (Editions Barthelemy).

* * *

A place, a time: Sampling lavender honey from the Valensole plateau is a treat no matter where you do it, but it's even better when do so right where it was made. Drive down the little roads on the plateau between Riez and Manosque or Manosque and Saint-Croix or toward Puimoisson. Stop at some quiet spot, admire the landscape, eat a spoonful of honey, and close your eyes. Unforgettable . . .

How to use honey? It's best all by itself. But it's also great in cakes, as a sweetener for tea, or at breakfast on toast . . .

CONFECTIONERY

For me, the world of confectionery evokes childhood, and life lived at a leisurely, unhurried pace.

At the same time, it's also a world that requires the discipline and precision of a jeweler. Childhood evokes a time of freedom when the future has not yet begun to call, when the present moment reigns supreme, and flavors breach its boundaries at will.
We wolf down childhood like a special treat, and it's true that the memory of those tender instants has returned to me ever since—inevitably. Sweets in general also represent moments that are relaxed and unhurried. I can't imagine gobbling down a piece of chocolate or cake in haste, simply because, at that stage in the meal, the appetite is tamed, sated.
It can also be a moment of trespass, of gratuitous self-indulgence, an instant "rendered unto sin," as Georges Bataille puts it.

Where to find the sweets of Provence...

Carpentras (Vaucluse). ✳The best place to buy candied fruit is from the Confiserie Bono, 280 Avenue Jean Jaurès (04.90.63.04.99)✳ where this delicacy—and a wide selection of jams—is made on the premises.

✳Maison Jouvaud, confectioners' and pastry shop, 40 Rue de l'Evêché (04.90.63.15.38)✳ Founded in 1951, and definitely one of the best confectionery-pastry shops in Provence. A warm welcome, homemade chocolates that regularly win first prize in blind tastings at the celebrated Club des Croqueurs de Chocolat (Chocolate-Lovers Club) in Paris.

✳Gazoti, chocolates and pastry, 118 Rue de la République✳
✳Chocolatier Clavel, 30 Rue Porte d'Orange (04.90.63. 07.59) ✳ Coffee-flavored chocolates, chocolates with hazelnuts, chocolate truffles, hard candy.

✳Confiserie du Mont-Ventoux, 288 Avenue Notre Dame de Santé (04.90.63.05.25)✳ For their specialty, white-striped hard candy.

Gargas (Vaucluse). ✳Confiserie Saint-Denis, Quartier des Janselmes (04.90.74.07.35)✳ This is probably one of the best addresses in the region. Old-fashioned craftsmanship and a rare dedication in the production of candied fruit.

Allauch (Bouches-du-Rhône). ✳Le Moulin bleu, 7 Cours du 11 Novembre (04.91.68.19.06)✳ Taffy and honey-drops produced by the Brémond family since 1835. A house recipe based on lavender, glucose syrup, and sugar paste.

Aix-en-Provence (Bouches-du-Rhône). ✳Confiserie Brémond, Rue d'Italie (04.42.27.36.25)✳ Excellent *calissons*, the famous tiny sweet made from a paste of bitter (Provence) almonds and glazed with sugar. A treat!

✳Léonard Parli, 35 Avenue Victor Hugo (04.42.26.05.71)✳ Another outstanding address, renowned for the superb décor and homemade products of a house founded in 1874. Tours available by telephone appointment.

✳Chez Béchard, 12 Cours Mirabeau✳ A must for confectionery of every variety, plus cakes and pastry.

Marseille (Bouches-du-Rhône). ✳Les Clonies, 26 Rue Lulli (04.91.54.11.17)✳ Snacks and teas; jams, gingerbread and *petits fours*.

✳Biscuiterie Orsoni, 7 Boulevard Louis-Botinelly (04.91.34. 87.03)✳ Sample this shop's two specialties: the famed *navettes* and anis-flavored *canistrelli*.

Saint-Rémy-de-Provence (Bouches-du-Rhône). ✳Chocolaterie Joël-Durand (04.90.92.38.25)✳ Unusual creations featuring chocolates flavored with lavender, black olive, Camargue saffron, rosemary, and arbutus honey. 180 F per pound ($24).

✳La Roma, 33 Boulevard Marceau (04.90.92.14.33)✳ For the famous macaroons, and also for enjoying a dish of ice cream on the terrace.

Collobrières (Var). ✳Confiserie Azuréenne, Boulevard du Général Kœnig (04.94.48.07.20)✳ For the *marrons glacés* and Confectionery Museum.

Sisteron (Alpes-de-Haute-Provence). ✳Confiserie Siat, 19 Rue Saunerie (04.92.61.00.57)✳ Thierry Siat's almond nougat with candied fruit, pistachios, or flavored with coffee.

Tourettes-sur-Loup (Alpes-Maritimes). ✳Confiserie Floria, Quartier Pont du Loup (04.93.59.32.91)✳ Mimosa, verbena, violets, dwarf-oranges, chocolate-coated candied orange-peel, fruit paste, acid drops, crystallized flowers, jasmine jam, and much more.

Nice (Alpes-Maritimes). ✳Auer, 7 Rue Saint François de Paule (04.93.85.77.98)✳ A tearoom combined with a spectacular confectionery shop founded in 1820. Jams, caramels, candied fruit, etc.

✳Confiserie Mimosa, 27 Avenue Jean Médecin (04.93.88. 35.11). Candied fruit a specialty.

The taste of Menton lemons

Here in Menton, "one of the loveliest spots on earth," the lemon is like some carefully preserved planet's pole star, glowing throughout a history that from time immemorial has made it one of the city's key features. The apogee of the Menton lemon probably occurred during the nineteenth century, when the prince of Monaco (and also of Menton) granted a series of special privileges—such as the right to set prices—to the owners of small lemon groves. This was the era of the "lemon magistrates," who designated official lemon harvesters. The rules were strict: lemons could only be picked in fine weather, and only when dry. They had to be transported in cloth-lined baskets. When ladders were used, they were not allowed to damage the tree branches. Pickers could not wear shoes with cleats.

However, the advent of the twentieth century marked the decline of the lemon—due to early frosts, increased competition from around the Mediterranean, a decline in the rural population, and the development of urbanism and the tourist trade. **Very simply, by the 1920s lemons had virtually disappeared from Menton.** Séverin Capra's parents were produce farmers at the time. To give their son something to do and to "keep him off the streets," they gave him a plot of land on which to plant his collection of lemon seeds. He had about 45 pounds of them. Within just a few years, 12,000 lemon trees had sprung up on his land. Bowing to the inevitable, the father decided to form a partnership with the son. Today, 63 years later, Séverin has a magnificent view of lemon groves from his upper terrace. His own son, Vincent, has taken up the torch, and can read the story of his life writ on the strata of the hillside.

What varieties? Menton once boasted 9 different varieties of lemon: the common, the long, the Valencia, the Tahiti-lime, the Portugal, the Poirette, the Mela-Rosa, citron, and giant citron. Séverin Capra's favorite is the elongated, delicate-skinned Santa-Théresa.

Where to find the best lemons? At almost all regional markets, under the label *"citrons du pays"* or sometimes *"citrons de Menton."* ✱ At the Menton market, we recommend Philippe Catananzi (*"bord de mer"* or seacoast entrance) ✱ Plan on spending about 10 to 15 F per pound ($1.40–2.00).

Where to find the best lemon trees? ✱ In Menton, at Séverin and Vincent Capra's à Menton (04.93.35.99.76), for example ✱ From a low of 150 F ($20) to 2,500-3,000 F ($333–400) for 30-year-old trees.

A place, a time: to appreciate lemons in their natural habitat, take a stroll along the back roads above Menton, toward Castellar.

www.villedementon.com

My recipe for preserved lemons

2 lbs. large lemons, 4 tablespoons salt, 2 cups olive oil.

* Wash the lemons thoroughly, leaving them unpeeled. Cut into thin slices or quarters. * Place the cut-up lemons in a strainer, sprinkle with the salt, and allow to drain for 12 hours. * Pack the drained lemons in a mason jar and cover with olive oil. * Close tightly and allow to age in a dark place for 2 months.

Preserved lemons can be used as a condiment with fish, broth, and vegetable stews. Some lovers of roast chicken insert a slice of preserved lemon into the cavity of the bird before it is placed on the spit.

* *
 *

The taste of almonds

Almonds add a mild, sweet grace note to the regional symphony. Almonds are the white keys on a vibrantly colored keyboard. They can strike either a sweet or bitter chord. They cover a scale ranging from delicate and tender to semi-hard and hard. But that's not all. Almonds can also shift registers depending on the soil they're grown in. Tradition has it that almond trees will thrive in the poorest soil —the kind you wouldn't ordinarily think of using for anything, even "the toughest seeds," as Villeneuve noted in the early nineteenth century. This explains why the inventory of the French culinary heritage includes numerous varieties, beginning with la Dame de Provence, harvested when still green; the hard Béraude, for luxury chocolates; the Flour-en-Bas,

for luxury confectionery; the Flot, for luxury Jordan almonds; the Fourcouronne, for ordinary Jordan almonds; and the Gove Rose, for pastry and nougat.

Note, however, that almonds are not extensively grown in Provence, and that 60% of all local production is used for the manufacture of chocolates, nougat, Jordan almonds, cocktail nuts, and so on. Open markets are the best places to find Provence almonds. Ask for them by name, and look for the Princesse, one of the best varieties.

*
* *

Recipe for almond and lemon soup

1 yellow onion, 1 clove garlic, 4 tablespoons olive oil, 1 tablespoon flour, 6 cups light cream, 6 cups chicken broth, juice and grated rind of 1 lemon, pinch of ground nutmeg, 1 bay leaf, 3 tablespoons roasted slivered almonds, salt, pepper.

*Chop the onion. Crush the unpeeled clove of garlic with the back of a knife-blade or wooden spoon. Heat the olive oil in a large pot, add the onion and garlic, and brown slowly. * Sprinkle with the flour and cook over low heat for 1 minute, stirring constantly.
* Add the chicken broth and bring to a boil. Stir with a wire whisk to avoid lumps. *Add the lemon juice and rind, bay leaf, and nutmeg. * Season to taste with salt and pepper.
* Simmer covered for 20 minutes. Mix in blender, and pour into soup tureen. *Add the cream, whisking gently, and 2/3 of the almonds. Chill thoroughly.
Garnish with the remaining almonds and serve.

Recipe from "Terre Provençale," January 1997.

Avec l'âge
l'art et la vie
ne font qu'un

The taste of orange-flower water

Every year between April 15th and June 15th, orange flowers are harvested from the tree and taken to the cooperative.

They are weighed and then spread out in the sun — evenly, so as prevent damage. In preparation for the distillation process, leaves and stems are removed from the flowers before they have time to wilt.

The flowers are then placed in copper distilling vats, with 150 to 175 gallons of water added for every 450 pounds of flowers. When this mixture is boiled, approximately 150 to 175 gallons of orange-flower water is produced, in addition to 2 pounds of the oil that rises to the surface. This oil is known as néroli, a rare essential oil used in the manufacture of perfume and eau de Cologne.

As an herbal remedy, orange-flower water can be made into a tea (use about 1 ounce per day). Orange-flower tea is believed effective for the treatment of indigestion, insomnia, and muscular spasms.

An address: ✳ Le Nerolium, Avenue Georges Clemenceau,
in Vallauris (Alpes-Maritimes, 04.93.64.27.54) ✳
About 24 F per quart unbottled ($3.20), 30F bottled ($4).

VILLAGES

You'll see, it's a land of endless riches— grandiose, noble, heart-rending.

Our image of Provence is that of a land often slightly out-of-phase with reality —not necessarily a bad thing. Tourists tend to focus on the Riviera, its languid architecture and stunningly azure sea and sky. They have little time to spare for unspoiled nature, which in any case has often been destroyed by a relatively catastrophic urbanism.

What you should do is take your time, shed your preconceived ideas for a day, and embark on an exploration of the authentic, rural Provence. When you do, you'll discover a land of endless riches —grandiose, noble, heart-rending. Below is a list of villages that are truly authentic.

• VAR •

✳ **BARGEME.** Some road signs deserve a salute, a joyous toot of the horn. On the back road climbing toward the highest village in the Var (Alt. 3,500 ft.), there's a sign showing a bus with a red circle around it and a red slash through it. Tourist buses not allowed? Hey, this place must be special! At about 1 P.M. on a blazingly hot July day, the village is deserted. Not a soul in

the tiny, winding streets. No arrows pointing to shops selling lavender, leather bracelets, or handcrafted pottery. **Just rose-covered stone cottages, huge clumps of wisteria, and the azure sky shimmering in the heat.** The only door opening to the traveler's knock is a gîte rural offering home-stays. Madame Noël shows off her rooms. They're clean and cool, with views of a lush landscape locked in infinite silence. Outside, untamed nature watches over – keeps an eagle eye on – this village that once led a life that was depraved, to say the least.

The record is a harsh one, describing individuals of great cruelty and "formidable hatreds" active during the wars of religion (sixteenth century) that soaked Provence in blood. Intransigent fathers, sons cut down in the open street, their throats slit in the village's meeting hall. Dread and horror! The descendants of the Pontevès family were no exception to the rule. One of their own, at the age of 25, died of a stab wound at the foot of the church's main altar during Sunday mass. In response, throats in the parliament at Aix were also strangled, but with indignation, ordering the people of Bargème to erect a chapel dedicated to Notre-Dame-d'Espaïne (patron saint of fear and pain) and to build it at the end of the château's esplanade. Knowing this history makes it almost easier to understand the village's triumphant silence today, the redemptive peace that broods mutely over its "formidable" past.

How to get there? From Bargemon, via D25 and D37.

Accommodation: The village boasts a single *gîte rural*, containing 5 rooms with views of the tranquil and magnificent village.

The rooms are clean, cool, and decorated in an understated style touched with charm and breathing utter tranquility.

✳Madame Annie Noël, Le Village (04.94.84.20.86)✳ offers a warm welcome and does the cooking for her table d'hôte herself: spinach soup, pork *au gratin* with sage, etc.

Meals 90 F ($12) per person, wine and coffee included!

Rooms 300 F ($40), breakfast included.

Walking tours: endless choice. **Information:** 04.94.76.81.25.

✳ COTIGNAC. "The thing that makes me saddest," says the Tourist Office woman on the telephone, "is when people go through Cotignac without staying for a while." And it's true that few villages have as much to give as this one. Effortlessly, with an infinite pleasure projected naturally by its café terraces and fountains . . . . Here, people are in tune with time, they linger, letting the minutes—and even the whole day—pass by. The very air rings with good humor, echoed by vivid lavender shutters, the local accent, the chatter audible from inside the courtyards.

Cotignac is tangibly present, resting like a charm on its benches, its landscape. One of the loveliest bell towers in the region rises gracefully from the Place de la Mairie. Its refrain is taken up by the 16th- and 17th-century houses, some of them distinguished (as on the main street) by pretty caryatids. There's a kind of enchantment at Cotignac, a state of grace seemingly safeguarded by the utterly tranquil landscape enfolding it as one might enfold something infinitely precious.

How to get there? Take the Brignoles exit on A8. It's 16 miles to Cotignac, 23 miles to Draguignan.

The most scenic route: the Barjols road, now bypassing the village of Montfort, has better views than the Brignoles road.

Accommodations: ✳the Lou Calen hotel (04.94.04.60.40, rooms from 270 F – $36)✳, for its distinctive charm, its terrace, and its honest cuisine. You should also try ✳Les Sports, a bar-restaurant on the Cours Gambetta✳ A number of bed-and-breakfasts, including ✳Le Domaine de Nestuby, Route de Montfort, Quartier Nestuby (04.94.04.60.02)✳ and ✳Le Clos des Vignes, Quartier Nestuby (04.94.04.72.19)✳

A time, a place: in the morning, at about 7 A.M., take a stroll around the fountains, especially La Fontaine des Quatre-Saisons at the end of the Cours Gambetta. At the end of the day, wander over to La Place de la Mairie for a view of the rock face and the lights.

Tourist attractions: the old quarter, Notre-Dame-de-la-Grâce, the gallery-museum on the Rue d'Arcole, the Church of Saint-Pierre.

Market: Tuesday mornings. **Tourist Office:** 04.94.04.61.87. **Mayor's Office:** 04.94.04.60.01.

✳ SEILLANS. Sometimes Provence makes the idle stroller feel like a spoiled child. Ravishing landscapes open onto sweeping vistas, the scent of meadow-bloom and lavender is strong, one charming village follows another. While you're still under the spell of Moustiers-Sainte-Marie, Bargème, and Bargemenon, bing! Seillans emerges at a turn in the road. You think it's going to be as imperturbably charming as all the rest, but think again! Seillans is different.

There's more asperity in the tiny houses perched around the bell tower, the 11th-century church, and the medieval château. More commotion (real people, children at play) in this village currently up in arms over a decision by the French national electric utility (EDF) to install a high-tension line between Boutre and Carros. "Save our region!" reads a local petition. This is the kind of heated controversy underscoring the genuine singularity of a village that stopped Robert Doisneau and Max Ernst in their tracks. Ernst visited often with his wife Dorothea Tanning before settling here permanently in 1964. They purchased a typical old residence in the village and named it "La Dolce Vita." American art critic Patrick Walberg, who first brought the couple here, also describes Seillans: its "supernatural quality," "a projection invulnerable to the passage of time," "a setting that gives wings to reveries," "the kindness and gentle ways of the Seillans inhabitants, inherently proud and gifted."

All of which explains why we leave again almost regretfully.

How to get there? On A8, exit at the Andrets toll station, 21 miles from Grasse, 78 miles from Toulon. One of the most beautiful roads to Seillans is via Fayence.

Accommodation: try the family-style ✳Hotel de France-Clariond, Place Thouron (04.94.76.96.10, rooms from 350 F – $47), in the upper village✳ Just as good is the cozy and elegant ✳Deux-Rocs, Route de la Parfumerie (04.94.76.87.32, rooms from 300 F – $47)✳

A time, a place: to savor the heart and soul of Seillans, take a moment to meditate under the shady trees or in the Notre-Dame-de-l'Ormeau chapel (very fine carved 16th-century altarpiece).

Tourist Office: 04.94.76.85.91: open Thursday mornings from 10 A.M. Elisabeth Bouchard organizes ✳guided tours of Seillans✳

• ALPES-MARITIMES •

✴ COARAZE. Something special happens when you reach this medieval village located near the Mercantour nature park. At an altitude of over 2,000 feet, a direct route seems to open toward the sun and heavens above. The heavens, in turn, have sent down a rowdy cohort of 118 cherubim spreading their wings under the vaults of the 14th-century church. The sun shines so brightly that the church's façades have been studded with sundials — some existing in noble anonymity, others signed with famous names: Jean Cocteau, Mona Christie, Ponce de Léon, Valentin, Henri Goetz, Douking. But the best thing about Coaraze is a sense of calm seemingly suspended in time. True, the bends and curves in the long road no doubt tend to temper high spirits, but the fact remains that **strolling in this celestial spot darkened only by the furry shadows of the village cats is a rare luxury, a privilege.** We feel grateful for these unique moments spent in a village swept by gentle gusts of pure air. It's so simple. At nightfall, I found myself almost walking on tiptoes and was rewarded, in return, with a muffled silence, an extra touch of joy.

How to get there? The village is 30 minutes from Nice, by the magnificent road running from Nice-Est to Contes. The final miles of the journey are blissful.

Accommodations: if you're looking for someplace simple, friendly, and authentic, with rustic rooms opening onto stunning views and for a family-pension atmosphere with respectful courtesy and unobtrusive attention, you'll find it at ✴L'Auberge du Soleil, Place du Vieux-Village (04.93.79.08.11)✴ A perfect balance (from 100 to 200 F – $13–27). The menu is in the same style: simple, unpretentious dishes—which is quite rare (good wine list). Swimming pool. Another suggestion in the area ✴Ferme-Auberge de la Parré, 06390 Parré (04.93.79.32.03)✴

Local sights: Chapel of Notre-Dame-du-Gressier (the "blue chapel") and the Saint-Sébastien chapel.

At aperitif time: Les Arts, Place A.-Mari.

A bench in the sun: "Plaça do Portal," opposite the crucifix.

Special events: ✴Olive Tree Festival, mid-August. Chestnut Festival, October✴

Information: 04.93.79.37.47 or 04.93.79.34.80.

✳ GOURDON. You can often sense a village's inherent character as you approach it. Some villages appear suddenly, abruptly, as if begging to be excused for being too pretty, too fortunate. Others, and Gourdon is one of them, are unapologetic. When you take the Vence road, you have an uninterrupted view of rock face, peaks, cliffs. The road twists and turns, underscoring its attractions, showing off its panoramas. And they are truly magnificent here, on a stretch of over 50 miles running along the Riviera. The foot of the village offers a golden opportunity to stop and survey this fortified town dominating the Loup Valley. It boasts an 11th-century château, a cool and tranquil church, and a maze of tiny streets. The village's promotional brochure aptly explains its dual character: **the "Côte d'Azur" Gourdon, with its gaudy shops, and the more genuinely Provençal Gourdon, living its secret life in narrow back streets and alley-ways** —an elegant way of glossing over the "Mont-Saint-Michelized" entrance to the village with its souvenir vendors and pedestrian-traffic jams. **But we all know how to avoid the mob:** take the side streets, wait for the times of day when business is slowest, and the tourist buses leave. It is then that the village speaks with its own voice, reverberating with the distant ring of history.

How to get there? Gourdon is about 8 miles from Grasse, 16 miles from Vence.

The most scenic route: D2110 from Vence, or the Pré-du-Lac road crossing a vast oak forest after the arid La Sarrée plateau. You can also come in from the north, by the Caussols road.

Accommodations: there are no hotels in the village.

Restaurants: a few good ones, including ✳Restaurant du Vieux-Four, Rue Basse (04.93.09.68.60, from 80 to 110 F – $11–15, lunch only)✳ and, for its panoramic view, ✳La Taverne Provençale, Place de l'Eglise (04.93.09.68.22, from 80 to 120 F – $11–16)✳ and, for its panoramic view, ✳L'Auberge de Gourdon, at the entrance to the village (04.93.09.69.69, from 80 to 200 F – $11-27)✳ for deliciously simple cuisine: soupe au pistou, charlotte of lamb with eggplant . . . Very good!

Shops: there are many, but one of the best, ✳Sainte-Catherine, is located around a bend in the Rue de l'Ecole✳ and sells 35 varieties of vinegar, innumerable types of mustard, honey, jam, and olive oil.

Tourist Office ("Syndicat d'initiative"): 04.93.09.68.25.

* SAINTE-AGNÈS. When you exit the Nice-Genoa highway, a discreet sign points to the village of Saint-Agnès (about 2 1/2 miles away), "the highest coastal village in Europe." For a few minutes the road tangles with the complexities of the highway, weaving over and under it, and then the road goes up, breaks free, dawdles a little, straightens out-and comes to rest at last. We happened to arrive on a misty morning, to the sound of a studiously executed piano concerto drifting into the air above the postcard shop. **The streets were deserted, except for a little boy running home with a loaf of bread tucked under his arm.** The morning's austere shroud of mist turned out to strike just the right introductory note to the village of Saint-Agnès, which has stood guard over the Franco-Italian border since the nineteenth century. Saint-Agnès has always been a lookout post, fortified against bandits and pillagers through its hours of glory and solitude. In 1932, a fort (one of the best-preserved portions of the Maginot Line) was dug south of the village to protect Menton. Today the town has been peacefully converted by the writers, painters, and artisans living in its tiny lanes and arcaded passageways, affording a new and almost contradictory image to this paradoxical and extremely appealing spot.

How to get there? Sainte-Agnès is 5 miles from Menton.
Accommodations: two hotels vie for visitors' custom,
La Vieille Auberge, 92 Avenue de Verdun (04.93.35.92.02) and
Le Saint-Yves, Chez Tibert, 76 Rue des Sarrasins (04.93.35.91.45, rooms from 190 F – $25)
which also arranges room rentals in the village.
Local sights: The Maginot Fort (04.93.35.84.58), Espace Culture et Tradition
opposite the church, the site of the former château, the medieval garden, the historical trail.
Walking tours: Sainte-Agnès is a good base for
*hikes on Le Mont Ours (2,000-foot climb, 1 1/2 hours, magnificent view of the Mercantour);
the Pic de Garruche; the Pic de Baudon via the Col de la Madone
(1,140-foot climb, 45 minutes), with a view at the summit stretching
from St. Tropez to Corsica (in good weather)*
Walking tours start at the chapel. Recommended map: IGN 3742 Est (East), scale 1/25,000°.
Mayor's Office: 04.93.35.84.58. **Espace Culture et Tradition:** 04.93.35.87.35.

* **SAORGE.** The road leading to Saorge is impressive. The gorges cleaving the superb valley of the Roya are so narrow and steep they seem almost reluctant to let you pass. A mental picture occurs to you of this sheer landscape sharpening an imaginary wooden pencil and sketching a village with the point. That village is Saorge. The view from the road below is stunning and, for once, the tourist brochure has found an accurate comparison: **Saorge is reminiscent of a "Tibetan village."** Well worth a closer look, but don't expect toy-town pettiness or retouched-photo technicolor. Saorge is different. It's retained all the "good old" mountain ways, and doesn't make any particular effort to please visitors. Who cares? Take the local indifference to outsiders as an incentive to plumb the depths of this ancient fortified village and blend in with its stones — an experiment rewarded by an immediate sense of history. Because of its location and numerous fortified castles, Saorge once served as a strategic outpost on the first great "imperial" route traveled by the county's nobility to reach their lands in the Piedmont.

How to get there? Exit Nice via D2204 (Col de Braus, Col de Brouis) and take RN 204 to Fontan (a long road but a beautiful one). Exit Menton via D2566 and the Col de Castillon and Col de Brouis to Fontan. A short cut: via Ventimiglia, Breil-sur-Roya and RN 204 to Fontan.

Restaurants: *Pizzeria Lou Pountin with its small terrace, 56 Rue du Lieutenant-Jean-Revelli (04.93.04.54.90)* or the more traditional *Le Bellevue (dining room with stunning panoramic view), 5 Rue Louis-Perissou (04 93 04 51 37)*

Local sights: Saint-Sauveur church, for its Virgin and Child (1708) and carved portal. The monastery and its arcaded courtyard, its small cloister, and the Poggio Madonna. On Fridays, at the entrance to the village, opposite the bookstore and public phone booth, the Jardins de Ciastré holds a small market featuring mountain-grown vegetables: eggplant, zucchini, zucchini blossoms, basil, homemade *pistou*, etc.

Mayor's Office: 04.93.04.51.23.

WALKING TOURS

• • •

Curiously, the image most people have of Provence
is static. Horizontal. They picture Provence under
a hot sun at siesta time, lying motionless amid the
fragrances of its arid hills. In a sense, they wish it
would stay that way forever, like a bride photographed
on the steps of the church. But the Provence I treasure
within me is mobile and alive. Vertical. Provence is
the play of fountains, the rhythm of winding roads,
the gentle roll of the sea, the life of the marketplace,
noise and laughter. This explains the close relationship
I develop with the land when I visit it on foot.
I love to explore, to choose my own as yet untraveled
roads, to drop everything and draw close to what I value
most —the countryside in its shifting solitude, its vivid
essence.
When I travel by foot, I achieve a genuine communion,
an affective bond bringing me closer to the substance
and flesh of Provence.

On the Island of Porquerolles ~7

✳ Scenic views ✳

La montagne de Lure, from Mont Ventoux (Vaucluse). Between Manosque and Sisteron, take N96 and D946, D53 (or D13, direction Forcalquier), and then D950 to Saint-Etienne-les-Orgues.

Jabron Valley, from La Montagne de Lure. Between Manosque and Sisteron, take N96 and then D946.

Les Baronnies, from the north slope of Mount Ventoux.

La vallée des Duyes (Alpes-de-Haute-Provence). Between Digne and Sisteron, a geological reservation. Take D3 from Sisteron to Digne, via Thoard (stop on the way at the excellent ✳Dufossez specialty-food shop and the Chez Favier bar-restaurant, 04.92.34.63.71)✳ Superb views, particularly of Les Monges as you exit Authon.

The ocher quarries, overlooking the village of Roussillon. From Apt, take N100 direction Avignon and turn off on D4 direction Roussillon.

Le Verdon gorges. Take D952 between Moustiers-Sainte-Marie and Castellane to enjoy the scenic view aptly named "Point Sublime."

Long lake, Vallée des Merveilles. From Nice, take A8 direction Ventimiglia, then D20 and N204 through La Roya valley. At Saint-Dalmas-de-Tende, turn off to the Vallon de la Minière.

Cap Canaille. Take D559 from Marseille direction Cassis. After Cassis, take D141 to Cap Canaille.

Les Baux valley, take D17 from Arles and Salon-de-Provence, then D17 and D5 to Saint-Rémy-de-Provence.

Massif des Maures, on A8 between Hyères and Fréjus, exit Le Muy direction Sainte-Maxime.

Mirabel-aux-Baronnies, D938 from Nyon direction Vallée de l'Ouvèze via Buis-les-Baronnies, then D546 and D64 to Col de Soubeyrand.

✳ Sites of special interest ✳

Manosque (Bouches-du-Rhône). ✳Jean Giono House, Colline du Mont-d'Or. Tours Fridays from 2:30 P.M. to 5:30 P.M. by appointment, on request to the *Association des Amis de Jean Giono* (04.92.87.73.03)✳, which also organizes walking tours featuring spots frequented by the writer.

Marseille *calanques* (Bouches-du-Rhône). For a hike around the fjord-like inlets of Marseille lasting 3 1/2 hours (6.25 miles; 1,170-foot climb) leave the port of Callelongue and follow the GR 98/51 arrows direction Marseille-Veyre. ✳Information on the best hikes in the area available from the tourist offices at Collobrières (04.94.48.08.00) and Marseille (04.01.13.89.00)✳

Château Romanin (Bouches-du-Rhône). At Saint-Rémy-de-Provence, on the Cavaillon road, spectacular wine cellars on a site first discovered seven centuries ago by the Knights Templar. Take N7 from Avignon or Salon-de-Provence, exit Plan d'Orgon and take D99 direction Saint-Rémy. Tours at 11:30 A.M., 3:30 P.M. and 5:30 P.M. ✳Information: 04.90.92.45.87✳

Villa de Noailles (Var). Designed in 1925 by architect Robert Mallet-Stevens for Charles and Marie-Laure de Noailles. The list of those who once stayed at the villa includes Chagall, Aragon, Cocteau, Picasso, Dali and Buñuel. ✳Parc Saint-Bernard, above Noailles at Hyères. Information: 04.94.12.70.63✳

Carluc Priory (Alpes-de-Haute-Provence). On the Forcalquier road (N100) direction Avignon, just before Céreste. An ancestral spot in untamed natural surroundings that, despite continual pillaging, has preserved the meditative grace of stone arches and columns.

Château-Arnoux (Alpes-de-Haute-Provence). Walking tour from the Saint-Jean chapel belvedere, with an exceptionally fine view of the Durance valley and Lure mountain. ✳Information: 04.92.64.02.64✳

Laghet Sanctuary (Alpes-Maritimes). In this unadorned chapel located on the road between Turbie and the Le Paillon valley, more than 4,000 ex-votos reflect a tale of lives saved since 1652. To get there, take A8 direction Italy, then exit 57 (Turbie) direction Laghet, which is located around one of the innumerable bends in the road. ✳Information: 04.92.41.50.50. Small museum attached (open 3:30 P.M. to 5:00 P.M. except Tuesdays)✳

Menton (Alpes-Maritimes). ✳Villa Fontana Rosa✳ On the banks of Garavan Bay, a magical spot with its wild garden, ceramic benches, columns, and rotundas.

Fournel Valley silver mines (Hautes-Alpes). From Gap via N94 to Argentière-la-Bessée (open daily from June through September). The mines remained in operation until the nineteenth century and employed up to 500 miners. ✳Trips by horseback through the Provençal countryside. Cap Rando at Lauris (04.90.08.41.44)✳

Canal du Midi. Start from the Rhône River (Châteauneuf-du-Pape, Avignon, Arles, Camargue, Aigues-Mortes), then take the Canal du Midi for fine excursions through Provence.

The Pignes train from Nice to Digne. A trip featuring over 60 artful constructions, including 25 tunnels, 16 viaducts, and 15 bridges. Four departures daily. ✳For information, Chemins de fer de la Provence, 4 bis, rue Alfred-Binet, Nice (04.93.82.10.17)✳

✳ Following in the footsteps of... ✳

Ben. True, the house is not open to visitors, but if by chance you pass this way, spare a glance for the home of this conceptual artist, at ✳103 Route de Pancrace ✳, on a hillside of **Nice** (Alpes-Maritimes). An inscription on the door reads, "Chez Malabar et Cunégonde."

Paul Cézanne. At Aix-en-Provence (Bouches-du-Rhône). ✳Cézanne Studio, 9 Avenue Paul-Cézanne (04.42.21.06.53, open daily)✳ The studio, now open to the public, remains just as Cézanne left it. Also of interest, the ✳Granet Museum, 13 Rue Cardinale (04.42.38.14.70)✳ one whole gallery devoted to Cézanne. And be sure to try the ✳Paul Cézanne walking tour (map available from tourist office, 04.42.16.11.61)✳, which leads to the house where the artist was born (28 Rue de l'Opéra), and the school he attended (Collège Royal Bourbon, Rue Cardinale—now the Lycée Mignet), by way of the Torse riverbank, the Café des Deux Garçons, etc.

Marc Chagall. At Nice (Alpes-Maritimes), the Musée du Message Biblique, Avenue du Docteur-Ménard (04.93.53.87.21, closed Tuesdays)✳ surrounded by olive and cypress trees. Displays 17 monumental biblical paintings. **At Vence,** where Chagall lived, the artist willed a mosaic to the Eglise de la Nativité.

Jean Cocteau. Cocteau traveled everywhere, and went particularly often to **Coaraze** (Alpes Maritimes), where he designed the admirable sundial visible on the façade of the Town Hall. And to **Menton** (Alpes Maritimes), of course—the Town Hall's wedding-reception room is decorated with one of his frescoes and also inherited his *Les Deux Mariannes.* Be sure to visit the ✳Cocteau museum, in the fortified Vieux Port (04.93.57.72.30)✳

Colette. It was **in Saint-Tropez** (Var), at the ✳Villa Treille-Muscade✳, that Colette fell under the charm of this little port.

Alphonse Daudet. ✦Château de Montauban, **at Font-vieille** (Bouches-du-Rhône)), Rue de Montauban (open daily from April 1st through September 30th)✦ Daudet once stayed here, and the château displays a collection of relevant manuscripts, books, and photos. Also worth a visit ✦Moulin de Daudet, 1.25 miles from Fontvieille (04.90.54.60.78, closed in January)✦ displaying items that belonged to the writer. A pretty site from which Daudet drew inspiration.

Jean Giono. ✦Centre Jean Giono, 1 Boulevard Elémir-Bourges (04.92.70.54.54)✦ **in Manosque** (Alpes-de-Haute-Provence). Photos and manuscripts once belonging to the author of *Le Hussard sur le Toit*. Also in Manosque, the ✦Jean Giono house and museum on Les Vraies-Richesses hill (04.92.87. 73.03)✦ where Giono lived from 1929–70. It is on the rooftops of Manosque that the author's "hussar" walked, and Giono himself lived in various houses on the ✦Grande Rue (Nos. 2, 14 and 18)✦

Fernand Léger. In Biot (Alpes-Maritimes), a very fine ✦museum at 255 Chemin du Val de Pôme (04.92.91.50.30)✦ devoted to works by Léger, including two impressive mosaics (*Les Constructeurs*) measuring 500 sq. meters and 280 sq. meters, respectively, and one entire floor displaying tapestries, mural art, and ceramics.

Maeght. ✦Fondation Maeght, 623 Chemin des Gardettes (04.93.32.81.63)✦, **in Saint-Paul-de-Vence** (Bouches-du-Rhône): one of the most appealing museums on the Côte d'Azur, designed by Aimé Maeght, with works by Miró, Chagall, Braque (stained-glass windows in the chapel), Pol Bury, Tapiès.

Matisse. In the center of an olive grove at the Jardins de Cimiez **in Nice** (Alpes-Maritimes), the ✦Matisse museum, 164, Avenue des Arènes de Cimiez (04.93.81.08.08, closed Tuesdays)✦ contains a large collection of the painter's work: gouache cut-outs, preliminary sketches, sculpture, furniture, and personal possessions. **In Vence** (Alpes-Maritimes), Matisse designed and decorated the ✦Notre-Dame-du-Rosaire chapel and lived at a villa called "Le Rêve" from 1943–49✦

Mistral. At Maillane (Bouches-du-Rhône), the ✦Mistral museum, 11 Rue Lamartine✦ Furniture, paintings, souvenirs. **In Saint-Rémy-de-Provence** (Bouches-du-Rhône), another fine memorial to Mistral's life can be found at the ✦Musée des Alpilles, located in the Hôtel Mistral de Mondragon, Place Favier (04.90.92.08.10)✦

Marcel Pagnol. The town of **Aubagne** (Bouches-du-Rhône) honors the author of *Le Château de ma mère* with ✦le Petit Monde de Marcel Pagnol, Esplanade Charles de Gaulle (04.42.84.10.22)✦ and displays a diorama illustrating Marcel Pagnol's work with santons (miniature terra-cotta figurines typical of the region).✦The Aubagne tourist office (04.42.03. 49.98)✦ also organizes guided tours (groups only) to the locations where Pagnol's films were shot and the real places associated with his childhood memories. In a similar vein, there is also a ✦walking tour of Aubagne and the surrounding hills (from July 1st through September 15th)✦ with an explanatory brochure. Also worth a visit: the ✦Musée Provençal du Cinéma, 64 Rue Juliette, **in Marseille** (04.91.90.24.54)✦

Picasso. In Vallauris (Var), ✦Musée Municipal du Château, Place de la République (04.93.64.16.05, closed Tuesdays)✦, featuring *Guerre et Paix* (*War and Peace*). The Catalonian artist was fascinated by the art of ceramics, and lived at a villa named "La Galloise" in Vallauris for several years. **In Antibes** (Alpes-Maritimes), the ✦Château Grimaldi houses a Picasso museum (04.92.90.54.20, closed Mondays)✦ Large, cheerful frescoes, faun-musicians, reclining nudes, photos by Brassaï, Capa, and Villers, plus galleries devoted to Magnelli, de Staël, and Max Ernst.

Raimu. At Cogolin (Var), the ✦Espace Raimu, 18 Avenue Georges Clemenceau (04.94.54.18.00)✦ The famed actor's granddaughter has here assembled an evocative collection of props from Raimu's films.

Van Gogh. In Saint-Rémy-de-Provence (Bouches-du-Rhône), the ✦Hotel Estrine, Rue Estrine (04.90.92.34.72)✦ displays a number of documents relevant to Van Gogh. ✦Hikes and walking tours mapped by the tourist office (04.90.92.05.22)✦

Avignon (Vaucluse). ✦Petit-Palais Museum, Place du Palais-

• *Previous pages: ceramic by Fernand Léger (1952), on the terrace of La Colombe d'Or.*

The Chapel of Peillon ↝

✷ Museums ✷

des-Papes (04.90.86.44.58, closed Tuesdays)✷ Medieval and Renaissance works: Botticelli, Carpaccio, Giovanni di Paolo, plus the Campana collection.

Ménerbes (Vaucluse). ✷Musée du Tire-Bouchon (corkscrews), Domaine de la Citadelle (04.90.72.41.58, open daily during the summer)✷ The La Citadelle wine-growing estate displays over 1,000 corkscrews, plus estate vintages (available for sale) just waiting for this crucial accessory to release their bouquet.

Aix-en-Provence (Bouches-du-Rhône). ✷Musée Granet, Place Saint Jean de Malte (04.42.38.14.70, closed Tuesdays)✷ Archeology, primitive works from the Avignon region, Italian and Flemish art, and outstanding galleries devoted to European art and Cézanne, respectively.

Arles (Bouches-du-Rhône). ✷Muséon Arlaten, 29 Rue de la République (04.90.93.58.11)✷ An ethnographic museum featuring the history of life in Provence.

Les Baux-de-Provence (Bouches-du-Rhône). ✷Musée Yves-Brayer, Hôtel des Porcelets (04.90.54.36.99, closed Tuesdays and in January and February)✷ During the 1950s this artist lived in Les Baux, where the canvases on display were painted.

Graveson (Bouches-du-Rhône). ✷Musée des Arômes et des Parfums (perfumes and fragrances), la Chevêche, Petite Route du Grès (04.90.95.81.55)✷ Retorts, a perfumer's console, bottles and jars, plus some fine Lalique glass. Garden featuring aromatic plants.

Marseille (Bouches-du-Rhône). ✷Musée de la Faïence, (ceramics) château Pastré, 157 Avenue de Montredon (04.91.72.43.47)✷ Three Marseille museums have consigned their ceramic collections to this superb 19th-century "country château."

✷Musée de la Mode (fashion), 11, la Canebière (04.91.56.59.57)✷ Renovated by Jean-Michel Wilmotte, this handsome residence holds fashion exhibitions. Museum shop and café.

Château-Gombert (Bouches-du-Rhône). Less than five miles from Marseille, a ✷museum of Popular Arts and Traditions typical of the Marseille region, 5, place des Héros, 13th Arrond (04.91.68.14.38, closed Tuesdays)✷ A reconstructed kitchen, formal clothing, furniture, ceramics, *santons* (miniature terra-cotta figurines), and nativity scenes. An appealing evocation of Provençal customs and traditions.

Tarascon (Bouches-du-Rhône). ✷Musée Charles Deméry

Souléiado, 39 Rue Proudhon (04.90.91.08.80, Mondays through Fridays, by appointment only)✷ For lovers of fabrics, old-fashioned cottons, and the costumes and ceramics of Provence. A delightful experience.

Saint-Tropez (Var). ✷Musée de l'Annonciade, Place Grammont (04.94.97.04.01, closed Tuesdays and in November)✷ An outstanding collection, including works by Utrillo, Seurat, Signac, Matisse, Dufy, Braque, Bonnard.

Volx (Alpes-de-Haute-Provence). ✷Ecomusée du Savon (soap), les Fours-à-Chaux (04.92.79.39.00)✷ Operated by the Occitane company, shop and small museum displaying posters, antique molds and machines.

Valensole (Alpes-de-Haute-Provence). ✷Musée Vivant de l'Abeille (bees), Route de Manosque (04.92.74.85.28, Wednesdays throughout the year, plus Fridays in summer)✷ Old photographs, beehives, apiary equipment, and an active hive available for viewing (protective precautions taken).

Moustiers-Sainte-Marie (Alpes-de-Haute-Provence). ✷ Ceramics Museum, Place du Presbytère (04.92.74.61.64, closed Tuesdays and from November 1st through March 31st)✷ Founded by Marcel Provence. A fine collection of items from local workshops famed since the eighteenth century.

Villeneuve-Loubet (Alpes-Maritimes). ✷Museum of the Culinary Arts–Auguste Escoffier Foundation, 3 Rue Auguste Escoffier (04.93.20.80.51, closed Mondays)✷ The famous chef who invented peach melba (named after diva Nelly Melba) is honored in the house where he was born with an extensive collection of menus, documents, and objects of culinary interest.

Saint-Jean-Cap-Ferrat (Alpes-Maritimes). ✷Ephrussi de Rothschild Museum, at the entrance to the cape, 1 Avenue Ephrussi de Rotschild (04.93.01.33.09)✷ An elegant house formerly known as the "Villa Ile-de-France," surrounded by magnificent gardens designed around various themes: Florentine, Spanish, Exotic, Japanese, French, and so on.

Monaco. ✷Oceanographic Museum, Avenue Saint Martin ([377]93.15.36.00)✷ A spectacular one-of-a-kind museum, with aquarium, whale skeleton, and much more. Stunning!

Ansouis (Vaucluse). ✷Château d'Ansouis (04.90.09.

✳ Gardens ✳

82.70)✳ Spectacular plantings of boxwood, hackberry, lilac, Judas trees, and pines bordering two gardens named, respectively, "Paradise" and "Secret."

Bouc-Bel-Air (Bouches-du-Rhône). ✳Jardins d'Albertas (04.42.22.10.25, daily from 3:00 P.M. to 7 P.M. June through end of August, weekends from 2:00 P.M. to 6 P.M. September and October)✳ Superb terraced French garden designed in the eighteenth century. Grand canal, fountains, statues of Neptune.

Puyricard (Bouches-du-Rhône). ✳Jardin de la Gaude, aux Pinchinats, Route des Pinchinats (Madame Beaufourt, 04.42. 21.64.19, by appointment)✳ A listed historical monument, this garden is famous for its boxwood maze, clipped yew trees, and butterfly-hunt path.

Hyères (Var). ✳Parc Saint-Bernard and Villa de Noailles Garden, Noailles hill (04.94.35.90.65, open daily)✳ Gardens and terraces overlooking the islands. Very fine, especially the "cubist" garden designed by Guévrékian in 1926. The Villa de Noailles, designed by Robert Mallet-Stevens for Charles and Marie-Laure de Noailles, is also open to the public.

Mane (Alpes-de-Haute-Provence). ✳The Salagon Priory gardens (04.92.75.70.50, open daily)✳ Notable for its Haute-Provence ethnological-heritage collection, and also for its medieval garden. Museum shop, bookstore, garden center.

APERITIF TIME

* * *

Pastis: in praise of slowing-down

Like everyone else who's swamped with work, I'm always ready to take a little time off. You can usually find a free moment if you really want to. One of my favorite moments is Pastis time.

Just thinking about it summons up a vision of cloudless Provence. The weather is warm, it's good to be alive, it's Provence.

A sip of Pastis brings back memories. The tide of time rolls in, submerging everything, changing everything, turning the world upside down. I love the sound of ice cubes against the side of the glass. The way they chink and click, slither and slosh! But a word to the wise: don't drown your Pastis in water, just a splash will do.

I'd rather drink Pastis than talk about it. But I do observe a few rules. First, the right company (no bores, grumps, or dullards). And then the right village (I'm not really a city person), the right café (not too crowded), the right chair and accessories-plump, flavorful black or green olives reflecting the tiled terrace, an ashtray placed like a paperweight over the check.

And the right glass, of course. I want one that's heavy, generous, plain. Large. Let's say it should be proportionate to the time-honored gestures of this ritual: throwing the head back as if preparing to launch a clarion-call, nudging the ice cubes with the tip of the tongue, feeling the liquid glide

down the throat. Ahhhh . . . !

If only time stood still. The leaves of the "platanes" are mistily visible through the glass. I hear a distant bell, villagers calling out, arguing, the conversation from the next table. Pastis is like the backdrop for a film, a blank page on which to inscribe Provence.

Another rule is to concentrate wholly on the business at hand, but let's not overdo it. You can also observe the activity in the square or, better yet, a game of pétanque— which would be perfect. Because it's at "Pastis time" that the sound of those metal balls rings out, that those imperious voices shouting encouragement, advice, prayers, and exhortations are heard.

Time to bend an elbow, engage in idle chat, catch up on the soccer scores perhaps, look and listen. But not too hard.

Sit back and enjoy the fragrances drifting on the air (mown wheat, lavender, eau de toilette on a shirt, the scents of arrested time, bread from the bakery, freshly watered gardens). Farniente time.

You see what I mean? You feel it? I'll leave you, now, to let you take your own time, to savor the moment.

* * *

Where to go at apéritif time

Aurel (Vaucluse). A pretty cliff-side village clinging to its church. When you leave the village on D942 direction Montbrun-les-Bains, stop at ✳that charming terraced café✳ on a lonely bend in the road.

Cavaillon (Vaucluse). ✳La Fin de Siècle, 42 Place du Clos (04.90.71.28.85)✳ An old-fashioned brasserie solidly projected into the present, with décor, moldings, and light fixtures that have earned its well-deserved rank as a listed historic monument.

L'Isle-sur-la-Sorgue (Vaucluse). ✳Café de France, 14 Place de la Liberté✳ Scene of the legendary photo (next page) by Willy Ronis.

Lourmarin (Vaucluse). Standing at a bend in the road, next to the Maison de la Presse, is a café where Albert Camus had his special table. In an effort to remain anonymous, he asked to be referred to as "Monsieur Terrasse."

Aix-en-Provence (Bouches-du-Rhône). ✳Les Deux Garçons, Cours Mirabeau (04.42.01.76.09)✳ *Farniente* at its best, watching the life of the city go by. Once frequented by Cocteau, Mistinguett, Louis Jouvet, and Mauriac—to name just a few.

Cassis (Bouches-du-Rhône). ✳Le Bar de la Marine, 5 Quai des Baux. (04.42.01.76.09)✳ Nostalgia in black-and-white on the walls, the brilliance of the daylight outside the door opening onto the port.

Marseille (Bouches-du-Rhône). ✳Bar de la Marine, 15 Quai de la Rive Neuve, 1st Arrond. (04.91.54.95.47)✳ For its admirable zinc counter, its terrace facing the port and the town hall . . . and its *aioli*, a Friday specialty.

Saint-Rémy-de-Provence (Bouches-du-Rhône). ✳ Café des Arts, 30 Boulevard Victor Hugo (04.90.92.13.41)✳ One of the best terraces in town.

La Cadière-d'Azur (Var). ✳Le Cercle des Travailleurs, 3 Place Jean Jaurès✳ An exclusive club also open to all, this bistro founded in 1883 has 200 provisional and honorary members who pay their annual dues before going on to relax in the distinctive 1930s-style bar.

Le Castellet (Var). If you're looking for genuine Provençal atmosphere, this is where you'll find it. Medieval streets, ramparts, and a lively population of artisans—the ideal mix to observe from a shady terrace. And there are plenty to choose from, such as ✳La Souco, 9 Rue de la Poste (04.94.32.67.94)✳ and ✳Mestre Pin (bakery), 1 Rue Tricot (04.94.32.67.94)✳Fabulous.

Saint-Tropez (Var). ✳Nano, 1 Place de l'Hôtel de Ville✳ or ✳Sénéquier, on the port✳ for taking the world's pulse at leisure.

Salernes (Var). On the banks of the Bresque, Salernes is famous for its natural-spring water—which makes your Pastis even better. The village is ravishing, featuring numerous fountains (notably the Fontaine de la Révolution, with its octagonal trough and stone grotesques). Our favorite terrace: the ✳Bar des Ormeaux✳

Seillans (Var). ✳Hôtel des Deux Rocs, Place Font d'Amont (04.94.76.87.32)✳Located in front of a fine 18th-century residence, facing the surrounding countryside. Relaxation and delight are on the program at Seillans.

Tourtour (Var). The name of this cliff-side village perched above Draguignan is appropriate to its medieval atmosphere. Old houses, arcaded passage-ways, and winding streets lead to the main square and the terrace of ✳La Fangoulinette✳

Lardiers (Alpes-de-Haute-Provence). ✳La Lavande café-restaurant, run by Emmanuelle Brollet, le Village (04.92.73.31.52)✳The name of this café alludes to its blue-tinted paneling, but the best thing is the village-bistro atmosphere underscored by tables outdoors, truffles and chanterelles mushrooms in season, a fixed-price menu at less than 100F ($13), and natural cuisine.

Manosque (Alpes-de-Haute-Provence). ✳Le Cigaloun, 10 Place de l'Hôtel de Ville ✳Under the "platanes," the terrace in Manosque, with a continuous street scene passing by in front, or ✳Glacier, 1 Promenade Aubert Millot✳ once patronized by Jean Giono, or ✳Le Grand Paris, at No. 3✳

Ongles (Alpes-de-Haute-Provence). Here you'll find the highest olive grove in the Forcalquier region, and a delightful village featuring wrought-iron balconies and plenty of shady arbors, such as the one at the ✳Café de la Tonnelle, le Village, run by Malvina and Marie (04.92.73.19.89)✳ Marie's *pissaladière* is definitely recommended!

Aspremont (Alpes-Maritimes). A village nestled in the hillsides around Nice, boasting the terrace at ✳Chez Mireille, Place Sainte Claude (04.93.08.00.12)✳

Biot (Alpes-Maritimes). ✳Café des Arcades, 16 Place des Arcades (04.93.65.01.04)✳ A distinctive spot with hotel, restaurant, and terrace attracting customers intrigued by an atmosphere combining contemporary art with the real Provence.

Castagniers (Alpes-Maritimes). Another spot in the hillsides around Nice (gorgeous road). Take D614 to the delightful little hamlet of Castagniers and the attractive terrace at ✳Chez Michel (04.93.08.15.15)✳

La Gaude (Alpes-Maritimes). On the Corniche du Var, 7 miles north of Saint-Laurent-du-Var via D118 and D18 stands La Gaude, its ancient castle of the Templars (sixteenth century), and the colorful and relaxing terrace of ✳La Guinguette, Chemin des Combes, Route de Cagnes (04.93.24.42.07)✳

Photo of the Café de France at L'Isle-sur-la-Sorgues, by Willy Ronis (summer 1979).

THE TASTE OF PASTIS

No less than 78 herbs and spices go into the composition of Pastis. The alcoholic content was fixed at 45° in 1938 by Paul Ricard. Apart from that, individual makers concoct their own recipes such as the one invented by Jean-Michel Berneau in Lacanau, for a Pastis similar in taste to absinthe.

Also worth sampling: Jean Boyer Pastis with tonka bean, Jean Boyer Pastis with artemisia, and Henri Boyer Pastis, all available locally.

✳ To accompany Pastis
- "La brissauda:" slice of crusty white French bread sprinkled with olive oil and toasted over a wood fire.
- "Lo capon:" a crouton rubbed with garlic.
- "L'alhada" or "aillade:" a paste made of garlic, parsley, salt and pepper.
- "L'aïoli..." the famous garlic mayonnaise.
- "La brandade de morue:" blend of puréed salt-cod and mashed potatoes.
- "Lo saussou:" sauce made from ground walnuts or almonds, garlic cloves, anchovies, olive oil, and verjuice.
- "Tapenade."
- "Eggplant caviar."
- Or with pistachios, olives, salted navy beans.

The address: ✳Distilleries et Domaines de Provence, Les Chalus, Forcalquier (Alpes-de-Haute-Provence, 04.92.75.00.58)✳
Pastis Henri Bardouin: made with 50 herbs and spices including artemisia, centaury, and sage; China spice (star anis), essence of badian; Indian spices, cardamom and pepper; South American herbs, tonka bean; maniguette from equatorial Africa; nutmeg and cloves from the Malaccan Islands; cinnamon from Ceylon. The distillery is not open to the public, but the adjacent shop-and-museum offers tastings and products for sale: Christmas liqueur wine, Rinquinquin, Génépi, Lure gentian, etc.

The taste of pissaladière

Today, it's pissaladière weather at the market in Old Antibes. Very hot. And here's Jean-Paul Veziano, sitting on a café terrace. While chatting with you, he's also steadily pumping the hands of passers-by. He's a municipal councilman and knows everybody. People keep stopping to say hello. But his true passion is his bakery. When he was mentioned in a national magazine as one of the best bakers in France, he reacted with the feigned amazement of a man well aware of his own worth.

What really gets him going —his abiding pride— is his pissaladière, an onion pie accented with pissalat (an anchovy condiment) and olive oil, garnished (sometimes) with anchovies and tiny black Marseille olives. He makes no secret of his recipe and willingly jots it down for us on a corner of the table. Rustic, popular dishes like pissaladière don't put on airs or go in for fancy pastry-work. No —what you see is what you get: a simple, crunchy crust that serves as a perfect foil for the filling. Yum!

No need to make a song and dance about it. Pissaladière speaks for itself, it's self explanatory.

How do you recognize a good pissaladière? The crust should be golden, the olives and onions should glow under their coating of olive oil.

A bad one? Underdone, too much oil, not enough oil, too many onions, too greasy, too much filling, bland and tasteless.

Onion warning: to make a good pissaladière, use yellow onions. White onions are too mild and watery.

A time, a place: one of the best ways to enjoy pissaladière is, first of all, to buy it from Jean-Paul Veziano. Then go sit on the terrace of one of the cafés in the Masséna market and order a small glass of rosé to go with it. Perfect for a snack around 11 o'clock in the morning.

The address: ✳Jean-Paul Veziano, 2 Rue de la Pompe, 06600 Vieil Antibes (04.93.34.05.46)✳

Jean-Paul Veziano's recipe for pissaladière

Quick and Easy!

the Antibes baker gives us his recipe:

2 lbs. plain bread dough, 3 lbs. yellow onions cooked in olive oil until soft and golden, 3 tablespoons anchovy paste.

* Stretch and pat dough into rectangular shape. * Combine onions and anchovy paste, spread evenly onto the rectangle of dough, and allow to rest for 30 minutes. * Bake in preheated oven at 425°F for 30 minutes.

• A variation:

1 lb. plain bread dough, 5 lbs. yellow onions, 4 cloves garlic, 1 small bouquet garni, 12 salted anchovy fillets (soaked in cold water to remove the salt), 24 small black olives, 1/4 cup olive oil.

*Place the olive oil in a heavy pot (to prevent scorching), add onions, garlic (outer skin removed, inner skin left on), bouquet garni. * Place over very low heat (a protective heat diffuser may be placed under pot). * Cover and simmer for at least 2 hours, stirring vigorously from time to time to prevent sticking and/or scorching. * When done, the onions should be fork-tender but unbrowned. If onions are not tender enough, continue cooking until done. * Stretch and pat the bread dough into a thin (3/4 inch), circular shape (use the hands, rather than a rolling pin) and form a rim to contain the filling. * Sprinkle a cookie sheet with water and lay the bread-dough circle on it. Allow to rise for 20 minutes while preheating oven to 400°F. * Bake the raised dough for 10 minutes and remove from oven. * Remove garlic and bouquet garni from the onion mixture. Spread the mixture on the baked bread dough. Garnish with the anchovy fillets and olives. * Return to oven and bake for an additional 15 minutes.

* * *

The taste of tellinas

If you've never yet seen a tellina, or sunset shell, you're going to melt at the sight of these tiny shellfish and their shimmering colors. Beiges, pinks, mother-of-pearl, pale blue . . . At aperitif time, warm tellinas are the ideal starter for a meal enjoyed under some shady arbor. These little bivalves, measuring just over an inch or so, are harvested in the Camargue, along the shore from Salins-de-Giraud to L'Espiguette beach at Grau-du-Roi, in Gard. Tellinas travel down rivers to the sea, sticking close to the sandy banks.

They live in whirlpools, frolic in fresh water. But the party's over when fishermen wearing waders collect them with their long scraper-nets.

That's when these little shellfish embark on a new career, and one that's just as colorful —featuring garlic, tomatoes, "rouille," and cream.

• **What about the sand?** To remove the sand, soak tellinas for 30 minutes in salted water. When they open, rinse repeatedly in clean water.

• **What wine goes with them?** A crisp, cool rosé . . .

Where to buy them? ✳ Mondays and Fridays at the Sainte-Maries-de-la-Mer (Bouches-du-Rhône) market, at Armand fish market, 13 Avenue de la République, and at the port between 9:00 A.M. and 11:00 A.M. when the fishing boats come in (look for Panpan on weekends) ✳

Mimi's recipe

2 lbs. of tellinas, 2 cloves garlic, 6 tablespoons olive oil, pepper, 1 bunch basil.

Remove sand (see above) and then allow the shellfish to open fully by shaking in an ungreased frying pan over moderate heat. Add the other ingredients and cook for 45 minutes.

The taste of socca

• • •

Today there's a long line in front of Thérésa's stall at the Cours Saleya market in Nice (Alpes-Maritimes). Out come the big copper platters containing her famed socca. It costs 10 F ($1.40) per slice —2 or 3 passes of the knife over the thin chickpea wafer, and then into the paper cone. OK, next!
Except that the people next in line are mostly tourists . . .
But that's the way it goes.

Some twenty years ago, socca was the local "Merenda," or morning snack. Laborers (and others) rising at dawn would sit on the wooden benches at Chez René, Les Caves Ricord, or Thérésa's, stuffing themselves with this little miracle. A small glass of red wine to go with it (these days it's rosé) and they were ready to face the day.
Everybody has their own way of eating socca. That's how it is with adaptable popular dishes like this one —it's good for breakfast, lunch, dinner, or supper; eaten seated or standing. . . But there are still some basic rules. Socca shouldn't be too thick or too greasy or too cold. You eat it with your fingers. And that's it!

The ingredients for socca are the same as for panisse: chickpea meal, water, salt, and olive oil. But everybody has their own proportions, their own oven temperature (a wood fire is best, but it has to be good, sound wood) . . .

Where to buy socca? At ✻Thérésa's in Nice, of course, 28 Rue Droite (04.93.85.00.04, closed Mondays)✻ Thérésa also has a stall at the Cours Saleya market. You can find honest soccas at ✻Chez René, corner of Rue Pairolière and Rue Miralheti✻ and at ✻Les Caves Ricord, corner of Boulevard Jean-Jaurès and Rue Neuve (near Le Café de Turin)✻, where they also serve pissaladière, pizza, Swiss chard pie, *pan bagna*.
Where to buy chickpea meal? ✻Chez Bertin, for example, located at 29 Rue Benoît Bunico, in Nice (04.93.85.76.53)✻, a grocery-store specializing in regional and organic products. The chickpea meal sells for 18 F ($2.40) per kilo (2 lbs.).

My recipe for socca

3/4 cup chickpea meal, 2 cups water, salt, olive oil.

Socca, like the Toulon specialty "cade," requires very little preparation.

The trick is to get the proportions right.

* Using the above ingredients, prepare a liquid batter (known as the "sauce"), as follows: place the chickpea meal and salt in a bowl, make a depression in the middle, and gradually pour in the water, stirring steadily with a wire whisk. Add the olive oil and continue stirring until a smooth batter (similar to crêpe batter) is obtained. Use immediately, as the batter turns sour fairly quickly. The batter is then spread in a thin layer on the special, large tin-platted copper platter used for baking because it distributes the heat evenly. If you don't have one of these platters, advises Franck Cerutti, my assistant chef at the Louis XV in Monte Carlo, you can use a Teflon frying pan with a metal handle. Bake the socca in a hot oven. * The oven should be very hot (wood-fired ovens can be heated to a temperature of 575° F). * Cook for 6 minutes, until the top of the crêpe is golden brown.

"You go into ecstasies when you see Gordes—that mountain redoubt drained of character by Parisian pseudo-intellectuals—because you've never been to Simiane-la-Rotonde (although the main highway goes right by it). You scoff at the charming little port of Cassis, that dreadful tourist trap, because you've never ventured as far as Niolon (Niolon is in the northern section of Marseille-Help!). You rave about a miserable bouillabaisse with crawfish served lukewarm in a corner of the Old Port, because you've never tasted gray mullet prepared by the fishermen from the calanques of Martigues. That's the problem of Provence today, in a nutshell. On one side you have the postcard-pretty cliché confected by effete "intellectuals," on the other side you have reality, life. And the thing that makes life interesting is that it's always on the move."

Philippe Caresse, "Terre Provençale," August 1998.

MARKETS

Market time is where it all starts, or goes on: the produce, the special dishes, the recipes, the local character. What we cook is inspired by what we find in the market. What starts out in the market ends up in the kitchen. Which is why the market is so important. The story opens at dawn, when we're still drifting between dream and daylight, not yet completely awake. But that's when we're at our freshest, just like the produce. It's the best time for getting the best choice. Later the displays will have been picked over by housewives, and even later by single men batching it on their own and infant-toting moms. Last come disheveled tourists with uncombed hair, who rush out at the last minute.

It's true that prices fall as closing-time nears, but so does quality. I hate to think of what goes into the baskets of late comers . . .

Here's how I do it. First I take a quick tour of the marketplace, making my selections and asking that they be put aside. When I've covered everything, I retrace my footsteps and pick up my purchases.

The time I spend making my quick tour of the market is a terrific thrill for me: I see everything, take it in, put it all together. I feel as though I have a whole culinary world at my feet, a tiny planet I can bestride, like Gulliver. Asparagus, apricots, tellinas, herbs . . . I cover whole regions, leap over rivers, climb mountains.

I'm intoxicated by the fragrance and freshness, the sights and sounds. The ideal method, for me, is to go to market early, return home to store my purchases and make preliminary preparations, and then return to the market (you always forget something —an herb, a vegetable), have a cup of coffee, read the newspaper, stroll around, chat with friends. Take plenty of time.

✳ A tour of local markets ✳

Nyons (Drôme). ✳ Market, Place de la Libération, Place Joseph-Buffaven and Place des Arcades (Thursday mornings) ✳ For olive oil, and also the excellent pizzas Chez Lulu—Mumu's aren't bad either. On the former Place aux Herbes, renamed Place du Docteur-Bourdongle, stands the Pâtisserie des Arcades (04.75.26.07.71) and, via the little back streets, Reflets de Provence, Place Autiéro (04.75.26. 26.00). Be sure to visit the Coopérative Nyonsais, Place Olivier-de-Serres, for its A.O.C. olive oil.

A good café: during the market or afterwards, make a stop at the Café de France, Place de la Libération.

A gourmet restaurant: Le Petit Caveau, 9 Rue Victor Hugo (04.75.26.20.21). Plan on spending 170–250 F ($23–33).

✳   ✳   ✳

Apt (Vaucluse). ✳ General market on Saturdays, farmers' market on Tuesdays ✳ The striking thing about this market is its diversity. Take a stroll through town (it's not very big), and admire the delightful mix of customers, from the most fashionable to the simplest—including the tourists, for whom souvenir stalls worthy of Saint-Paul-de-Vence have been set up. Among their many attractions (for those who might be a little hard-of-hearing): recordings of the local crickets. It's a short step from market stall to shop and back again.

Pasta: excellent lasagna from Pinna, Rue Eugène-Brunel, in some fifteen varieties (*pistou,* truffle, eggplant, etc.), plus dried pasta, tomato dried, and tiramisù "maison."

Fish: really good fish stalls are rare, but a highly recommended one is Meffre, in front of the excellent Dumas bookstore.

Meat: J.-C. Malavard, Place de la Poste, for prepared dishes and a good selection of meat.

Poultry: Caty and André Jehannin (from Bouvières) have a little stall above the Place de la Sous-Préfecture, opposite the Caisse d'Epargne bank, selling free-range chicken, pigeons, rabbits.

Vegetables: lots of low-cost stalls in the "Arab" market beyond Rue Pasteur. More expensive and somewhat farther away, Les Jardins de Saint-Anne, Rue Sainte Anne. Fine produce also available in front of the Dumas bookstore.

Truffles : stroll over by the Bistrot de France, Place de la Bouquerie, and you might run into Monsieur Bonis, who has plenty on display.

Fougasses (Provençal bread): Lou Fougassié, Rue Saint Pierre.

Cheese: 10 Rue de la Sous Préfecture. Wide selection of goat and sheep cheeses. Take a look at Elisabeth Murat's cheeses (Chèvredoux) and, opposite the Caisse d'Epargne bank, sample the products sold by La Maison Ricard (from Eygaliers).

Herbs and Salad Greens: Jean-Louis Danneyrolles, in a small street near the Sous Préfecture, who sells a range of salad greens including superb watercress, arugula, Raphaël Batavia, Moroccan cardamine, red lettuce, chervil, and blue-blossomed borage with that disturbing oyster smell!

Olive Oil: just about anywhere. If you come across the Cucuron variety, try it, it's very special. Otherwise, go for Saint-Saturnin oil. Near the poultry stall, also check out Dédé and Michel Faure.

Honey: Lydie, Claude Jeanne, and César, on the Place de la Sous Préfecture.

Candied Fruit: Confiserie Saint-Denis, run by André Rastouil, in Gargas (04.90.74.07.35).

Market bistros: everyone has their own habits and favorites. For us, Le Grégoire on Place de la Bouquerie has the most style. The others depend on personal taste—Le Ramponneau, Le Palais . . . the choice is up to you.

✶ How to get there: Apt is 31 miles from Aix-en-Provence, 33 miles from Avignon, 20 miles from Cavaillon. If you have the time, take the delightful road from Lourmarin (D943), which is a treat.

✶ Parking: a highly competitive local sport, but there's also a local secret—the dock-side parking lot, just before La Place de la Bouquerie.

Carpentras (Vaucluse). ✶ Friday and Saturday mornings for the organic market. A word to the wise: this market closes early, around 12 or 12:30 P.M.✶ If you like person-to-person interaction, joking around, and first-class produce, this is the market for you. Here's the real Provence, cheerful and voluble. This market has everything: the fragrance of jasmine, thyme, and marjoram; giant paellas and *churros;* chatter and laughter. Not to mention the local accent, which no one admits to—only the super-pedantic are tactless enough to mention it. In Carpentras, people kid around and get a kick out of life. They'll tease you, but they like you just fine. This is the realm of *estrambord,* a Provençal word meaning exaggeration, enthusiasm, tall-tale-telling with a wink of the eye.

Meat: Pons, Place Maurice Charretier, and Brunet Frères, Rue Vigne. And, for those who have developed a taste for horse meat, La Boucherie Chevaline, 13 Rue Vigne.

Salt Cod: in front of the town hall, not far from the olive seller.

Chickpeas: at the entrance to the market, Avenue Jean-Jaurès, a notorious spot . . . When the man behind the counter feels threatened, he can turn surly and devious (see for yourself!).

Truffles : from the end of November through the middle of March, Place Aristide-Briand, in front of the Café de l'Univers and the Café du Club. Need we mention that this region supplies over 75% of the total French truffle production?

Cheese: the best place to go is definitely the Fromagerie du Comtat (run by the Vigier family) on Place de l'Hôtel de Ville. Fine selection of cheeses and invaluable advice.

Bakery: try the regional specialties available at Allibert, 46 Rue Raspail. Quince loaves, *brassadeau,* and bread in every guise (country loaf, whole grain, etc.).

Olives: Rue de l'Evéché, right next to the Jouvaud *pâtisserie,* one of the best vendors in the market.

Olive oil: the one available in the market comes from Nyons (A.O.C.) and can be found almost everywhere, for example on

Avenue Jean-Jaurès at Rue de la Vigne (84 F, first pressing – $11.20).

Tellinas: for topping off the churros made before your eyes (a market ritual), "de-sanded" tellinas can be found at the entrance to Rue Porte de Mazan (35 F per pound – $4.70).

Nearby, two **booksellers** market their wares at the end of Rue du Saule.

Chocolates and Pastry: 40 Rue de l'Evéché (04.90.63. 15.38). Jouvaud (founded in 1951) is definitely one of the best confectionery-pastry shops in Provence, offering a warm welcome and chocolates "maison" that are regular award-winners at the blind tastings run by the famed Chocolate Lovers Club of Paris. A tea room prolongs the pleasure. Another excellent address: Gazoti, 118 Rue de la République.

Candied Fruit: The place to go is Confiserie Bono, 280 Avenue Jean Jaurès (04.90.63.04.99). Homemade candied fruit (including melon) and a selection of jams.

Coffee and Tea: Café d'Antan, 65 Rue Porte de Mazan. Fine selection of teas and coffees (roasted on the premises).

Garden Plants: At 93 Avenue Jean Jaurès, a wide selection of plants for your garden at home. Thyme, peppermint, citronella, chives, tomatoes, melons, etc.

Market Cafés: Le Bistrot des Palmiers, opposite the Palais de Justice; the terrace of Les Trois Brioches, Place Sainte Marthe; Le Richebar, Place de la République. Worth a visit, on the corner of Place de Verdun and the old Route de Mazan, a 1950s-style pizzeria also famous for its orange-flower fritters: a local ritual.

Velleron (Vaucluse). Market along the main road (late afternoons, except Sundays) As the road begins to peter out, you suddenly catch sight of a strange bazaar. A line of trucks, a crowd of people, and then—just the dull, deserted road again. So you back up and pay a visit to one of the most unusual markets in the region. It's a farmer's market that displays only produce harvested the same day. You get the picture: incredible freshness, cheerful vendors, low prices, and a fair deal right down to the bottom of the basket.

Potted Herbs: At the very beginning of the market (Stall No. 31), massive clumps of basil (15 F – $2), sage, and verbena (25 F – $3.40), thyme, chives.

Make your own walnut wine: stroll down to the end of the market and check out the lady on the right selling green walnuts (15 F a box – $2). She'll gladly give you her recipe: crack a few walnuts and place them in a quart of wine reinforced with alcohol. Add some sugar and cinnamon. Allow to macerate for about 40 days.

Mushrooms: the best display is the one on the right (stall No. 70). Chanterelles, boletus, meadow mushrooms.

"Baby Vegetables:" at the end of the aisle, on the right, tiny vegetables grown by a woman from Jonquerettes. Cucumbers, round zucchini, tomatoes, etc.

Poultry: Stall No. 138, free-range chickens, eggs, guinea hens, rabbits.

Summer Truffles: Stall No. 117. The display included plump apricots the day we were there, plus white truffles (45 F per box – $6) and . . . three little kittens whose mother, we were informed, is an accomplished witch.

Practical Extras: if you forget your market basket, you can pick one up at either end of th market (about 40 F – $5.50).

Aubagne (Bouches-du-Rhône). Cours Voltaire market (Tuesdays, Thursdays, Saturdays, Sundays) This is Pagnol country, as well as the capital of *santons* (miniature terra-cotta figurines) and olive trees. Here's the place to buy Brousse du Rove, the famous local goat cheese somewhat similar to ricotta.

Bar: Take your coffee break at Le Régence.

Buis-les-Baronnies (Alpes-de-Haute-Provence). In this charming village by the banks of the Ouvèze, a very special market is held every year on the first Wednesday in July. This is the lime-blossom market, where local growers offer fragrant bundles of the aromatic leaves for sale.

Sisteron (Alpes-de-Haute-Provence). Place de l'Horloge and Place du Docteur Raoul Tobert (Wednesday and

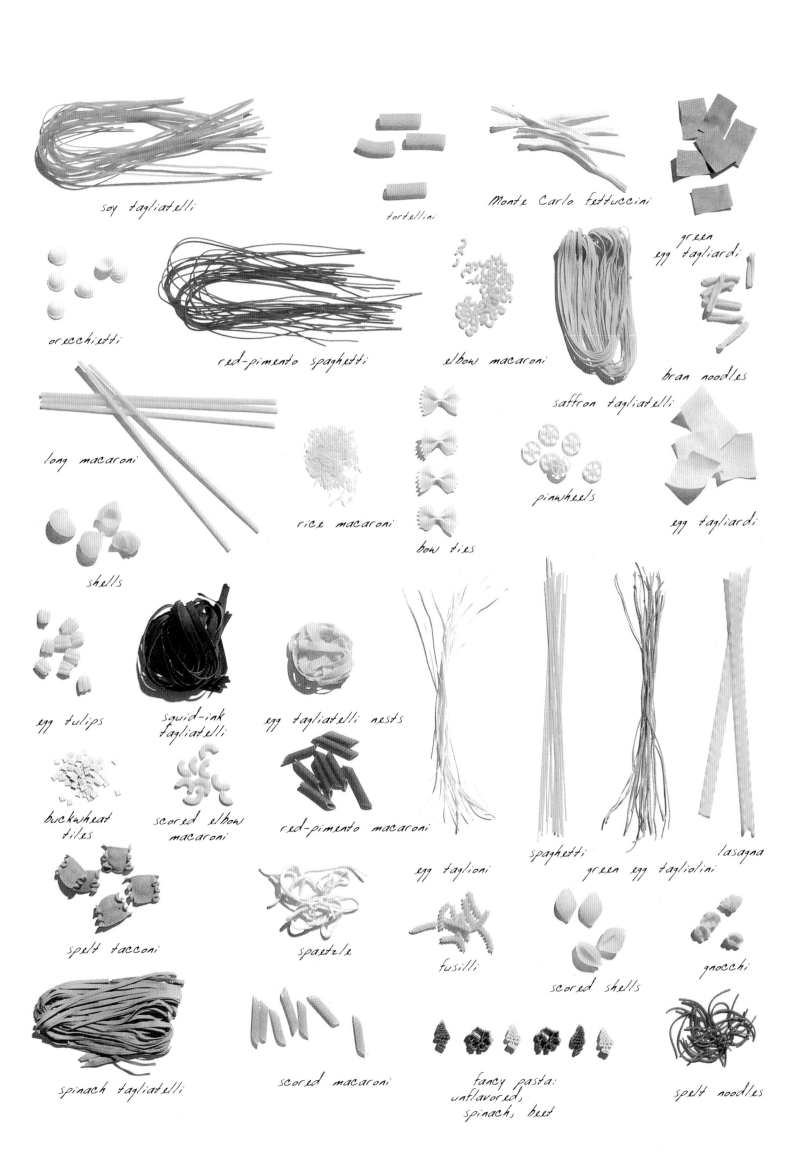

soy tagliatelli

tortellini

Monte Carlo fettuccini

green egg tagliardi

orecchietti

red-pimento spaghetti

elbow macaroni

saffron tagliatelli

bran noodles

long macaroni

rice macaroni

bow ties

pinwheels

egg tagliardi

shells

egg tulips

squid-ink tagliatelli

egg tagliatelli nests

buckwheat tiles

scored elbow macaroni

red-pimento macaroni

egg taglioni

spaghetti

green egg tagliolini

lasagna

spelt tacconi

spaetzle

fusilli

scored shells

gnocchi

spinach tagliatelli

scored macaroni

fancy pasta:
unflavored,
spinach, beet

spelt noodles

"While drifting
and dreaming,
you could
reconstruct
your whole life
around odors,
aromas,
and fragrances."

"Actually, buying pro-
duce in season
is one of the best
ways to get really
close to nature."

Saturday mornings)✱ On the banks of the Durance, for the quality of its vegetables and local specialties such as spinach, plum, apple and mashed-potato *tourtons* (pies)—Madame Seinturier's are the best—plus honey and gingerbread.

Antibes (Alpes-Maritimes). ✱ Antibes covered market (best days: Saturdays and Sundays; also open Tuesdays and Fridays, closes at 1:30 P.M.)✱ A real sweetheart. The odors, good humor, and gentle warmth projected by this bucolic construction give it a genuine Provençal flavor—exquisite, unforgettable. High quality is also a feature of the honest local produce, plus a few more exotic items. You should definitely take a stroll down the nearby streets and stop at the Veziano bakery for a *pissaladière* to enjoy on the terrace of a market café—another unforgettable experience.

Ravioli: at Perrin, 51 Rue Henri Lauguer (04.93.74.18.93), for fresh pasta and products from Italy.

Fresh Pasta: La Boîte à Pâtes, 5 Rue Sade (04.92.96. 96.78), one of Thierry Durand's five shops. Fresh pasta, prepared dishes, products from Italy, wine.

Vegetables: you'll find a wide selection in the center of the market at several stalls, including Madame Louise's (green beans, navy beans, etc.).

Potatoes: Jean-Marc Atard markets some 103 varieties throughout the year. Belle de Fontenay, mona lisa (for your gnocchi and mashed potatoes). Adjacent to Perrin's ravioli shop.

Poultry: Guy Ramouain, at La Boucherie des Alpes on the Cours Masséna, supplies all the classics, plus local products: Provençal salami, *porchetta*, prepared dishes (specialties from the Nice region).

Fish: The best place is Reine's stall, featuring fish from the local seacoast.

Cheese: The Fromages de la Montagne stall run by the faithful Jean-Pierre (good sheep's cheeses).

Pissaladière: from Jean-Paul Veziano, 2 Rue de la Pompe (04.93.34.05.46). Terrific! He also has Swiss-chard pies, natural-yeast baguettes, Corrèze bread, butter croissants, *millefeuilles*, apple pies, florentines, and other treats.

Bakeries: in Antibes there's Veziano, of course. And also Carlevan, 8 Rue Sade (04.93.34.78.46), featuring olive-oil

bread, Antibes-style loaves; Manganelli, 8 Rue d'Aubernon (04.93.34.54.72); and Mallamaci, 40 Boulevard d'Aguillon (04.93.34.73.29).

Pastry Shops: Les Canelous de Provence, in Jardins de l'Amiral, Chemin des Ames du Purgatoire (04.93.33.47.58), for its many original creations (particularly the Provençal *canelés*). Also note Le Palais des Friandises (04.93.34.47.14) at 50 Rue de la République, for the chocolates and desserts; and La Pâtisserie Cottard, 49 Rue de la République (04.93. 34.09.92).

Spices: Aux Cinq Poivres (04.93.13.02.97). Ask for Isabelle.

Olive oil: Balades en Provence, 25 Cours Masséna, and Crème d'Olive, 29 Rue James Close (04.93.34.08.55), where Bernard Lagier offers a wide selection of olive oils, olives, spices, and condiments.

Lavande: Martine Delaigne from Roquebillière (06.81.80. 03.32). Essential oils, dried flowers, and rustic bouquets.

Market Bistros: Bar Championnet, 33 Cours Masséna, and (early in the morning) Le Bacchus.

Market Restaurants: behind the ramparts on Place du Safranier, make a reservation at Le Safranier (04.93.34.80.50) for its Provençal cuisine (fish soup, zucchini fritters, stuffed sardines, etc.) and friendly atmosphere. Count on paying from 150 to 200 F ($20–27).

On the Cours Masséna, also try Chez les Poissonniers (04.93. 34.23.10) for its shellfish sautés, risotto, and dried fish. About 250 F ($33).

Nice (Alpes-Maritimes). Marketing on the "Saleya" is an experience you should try at least once during your stay in Provence, even if you only buy a pound of apricots or a handful of cherries. ✱ Mondays for the antiques and flea market, Tuesdays through Sundays for flowers and market produce. There are fewer small local farmers on Wednesdays—Saturdays are best✱ You'll soon see the difference. Small farmers fill the Place Gautier, and along the main aisle you'll see local merchants purchasing their supplies at the M.I.N. ("Marché d'Intérêt National"). If you want to buy from the farmers, you must arrive early (8 A.M.), since the best produce goes first, and fragile items (zucchini blossoms, for example) wilt quickly.

Vegetables: take a stroll through the market to find out where the best produce is. It's often on Place Gautier, at Morini's stall, especially good for lettuce, salad greens, chicory, sage. Go to Monsieur Jeannot for zucchini (and free-range eggs), or to Monsieur Dau for broad beans. Pizano's vast display features excellent potatoes. Ruggieri's salad greens are famous, but no one's going to stop you from looking around on your own.

Figs and Mushrooms: Definitely from Marie-Thé, in the middle of the aisle.

La socca: Thérésa, 28 Rue Droite (04.93.85.00.04, closed Mondays), who spends market days on the Cours Saleya. Chez René, on the corner of Rue Pairolière and Rue Miralheti; Aux Caves Ricord, on the corner of Boulevard Jean-Jaurès and Rue Neuve (near the Café de Turin), where you'll also find *pissaladière*, pizza, Swiss chard pie, and *pan bagna.*

Regional and organic produce: while you're at the market, stop off at Bertin (fancy groceries), 29 Rue Benoît Bunico (04.93.85.76.53). Chickpea meal goes for 9 F per pound ($1.20).

Little Cafés: La Civette, La Socca or Le Bar des Fleurs, all on the marketplace.

* * *

The taste of salad greens

We're on a plateau in the Lubéron, as if suspended between nowhere and the sky. The hour is radiant, the place extraordinary.

At the end of the road stands Jean-Luc Danneyrolles —a man with 12 years' gardening experience behind him— who is famous for his salad greens. His is a world of lovely fragility made up of dried flowers, old roof-beams dusted with pollen, cool barns, and the workshops where he arranges his bouquets and greens. This particular afternoon he's entertaining a group of children on a school field trip, teaching them the secrets of nature's bounty. The main subject is greens and the art of "composing" different mixed salads.

"It all depends on the season and the mood," explains our gardener.

"In winter, there are a dozen or so varieties with strong, crunchy notes, whereas in springtime everything is delicate and tender."

Today the greens are in flower. You might think the flowers are just a pretty extra, but you'd be wrong.

Try a bit of this blue borage blossom. At first you won't taste anything. But then, incredibly, you suddenly catch a strong flavor of . . . fish? . . . . of oysters!

Salad greens form an infinitely varied universe combining sweet, acidic, and bitter flavors, watercress with its characteristic zing, the subtle accent of chervil, the mustardy taste of arugula.

Even the names are evocative: red lettuce, ox-tongue, Moroccan cardamine, Raphaël Batavia, ice-queen, awl cress . . .

Close your eyes and open your mouth, and your ears.

How to serve salad greens: simply, with local olive oil (Cucuron, for example), a little salt, pepper from the mill, and lemon juice. Add burnet for its cucumber taste.

According to a Provençal proverb, "burnet may not cost its weight in gold, but gold doesn't taste as good as burnet!"

The address: ✴Jean-Luc Danneyrolles has a stand at the Apt market, on Saturdays, on a small street near the Sous Préfecture✴
In addition to salad greens (19 F for 200 g – $2.50), he also sells floral bouquets.

RESTAURANTS

Whether elegant or simple,
the great thing about these restaurants
is that no two are alike.

I find it hard to imagine traveling through a region without
stopping at a restaurant. This is the moment when everything
comes together. Now you can sit back and survey your surroundings
at leisure, while others cater to your comfort and pleasure.
A restaurant isn't just a plate and a glass. It's a whole
culture offering itself like an open book. No special comment
is necessary. Just a little idle conversation and quiet relaxation.
The great thing about these restaurants is that, whether elegant
or simple, no two are alike. Each sings its own special tune,
to a score accented with laughter and exclamations.

All the restaurants I've listed here sing the song of Provence.

However, when we decide to visit a restaurant, we often like
to have a very precise idea of what we'll find there.
That's why I've tried to note, for each of these addresses,
a distinctive dish well worth the trip.

* * *

✳ WHERE TO EAT WHAT? ✳

(For addresses and phone numbers not listed below, consult the list of restaurants by city.)

Angler-Fish (*baudroie*). Roast angler-fish with sautéed saffron bread and bourride, at ✳L'Auberge de la Fenière, Lourmarin (Vaucluse).

Beefsteak. Grilled, at ✳Los Caracolès, Aigues-Mortes (Bouches-du-Rhône).

Blood Sausage. Blood sausage *à la Niçoise* with potatoes, at ✳La Merenda, Nice (Alpes-Maritimes).

Bouillabaisse. ✳A L'Epuisette, Marseille (Bouches-du-Rhône). ✳Miramar, 12 Quai du Port (04.91.91.10.10), Marseille (Bouches-du-Rhône). ✳La Chanterelles, Port des Oursinières, 112 Rue Tartanne (04.94.08.52.60), Le Pradet (Var). ✳Restaurant de Bacon, Antibes (Alpes-Maritimes). ✳Au Roquebrune, Roquebrune-Cap-Martin (Alpes-Maritimes).

Bourride. ✳La Voile d'Or, Saint-Jean-Cap-Ferrat (Alpes-Maritimes).

Brandade. ✳*Brandade de morue* (purée of salt-cod/mashed potatoes), Chez Maurice Brun, 18 Quai de Rive Neuve (04.91.33.35.38), Marseille (Bouches-du-Rhône). Accompanied by dried tomatoes and pan juices, ✳Au Vieux Colombier, Dabisse-les-Mées (Alpes-de-Haute-Provence).

Burbot (*lotte*). Prepared *à la Niçoise*, ✳Chez la Mère Besson, 13 Rue des Frères Prodignac (04.93.39.59.24), Cannes (Alpes-Maritimes).

Calamari (*supions*). In shellfish broth, at ✳Le Château de la Chèvre d'Or, Eze-Village (Alpes-Maritimes).

Raviolis. Served in a salad with local navy beans, at ✳Bel Aqua, Hôtel des Etrangers, Sospel (Alpes-Maritimes).

Chicken. At ✳La Beaugravière, Mondragon (Vaucluse). Free-range chicken *en casserole*, ✳Chez Jacques Maximin, Vence (Alpes-Maritimes).

Cod (salted). Sautéed with mashed potatoes and olive oil, at ✳Le Fournil, Bonnieux (Vaucluse).

Crayfish (*langouste*). ✳Au Roquebrune, Roquebrune-Cap-Martin (Alpes-Maritimes).

Cuttlefish. With garlic, at ✳Le Charles Livon, 89 Boulevard Charles-Livon, Marseille (Bouches-du-Rhône, 04.91.52.22.41).

Farce. Ramekins of stuffing accompanying milk-fed lamb with thyme blossom, at ✳Le Moulin de la Camandoule, Chemin Notre Dame des Cyprès, Fayence (Var). About 100 to 300 F ($13–40).

Garlic. *Aligot* (garlic-flavored potato purée), at ✳L'Aligot, Place des Cardeurs (04.42.63.00.26), Aix-en-Provence (Bouches-du-Rhône). Aioli, at ✳L'Auberge du Port, 9 Rue de la République (04.94.29.42.63), Bandol (Var).

John-dory (*saint-pierre*). Baked, with calamari and violet artichokes, ✳Jean-Jacques Jouteux, Saint-Jean-Cap-Ferrat (Alpes-Maritimes).

Kidneys. Whole veal kidneys baked in a sauce made with red onions and Bandol wine, at ✳Issautier, Saint-Martin-du-Var (Alpes-Maritimes).

Lamb. ✳La Riboto de Taven, Les Baux (Bouches-du-Rhône). Shoulder-of-lamb dried. ✳Chez Bruno, Lorgues (Var). "Inferno-roasted" shoulder-of-lamb at ✳La Bonne Etape, Château-Arnoux (Alpes-de-Haute-Provence). Roast milk-fed lamb with tomato dried at ✳La Villa des Lys, Cannes (Alpes-Maritimes). With white beans, potatoes, tapenade, pine nuts, and almonds at ✳L'Auberge de la Madone, Peillon (Alpes-Maritimes). Rump of Sisteron lamb with fresh mint and white beans ✳Chez Issautier, Saint-Martin-du-Var (Alpes-Maritimes).

Lamb, leg of. Seven-hour roast leg-of-lamb, at ✳L'Oustau de Baumanière, Les Baux (Bouches-du-Rhône).

Lavender. Special menu at the hotel-restaurant ✳L'Aiguebelle, Place de la République (04.92.79.00.91), Céreste (Alpes-de-Haute-Provence).

Minestrone. With prawns and shellfish, at ✳La Réserve de Beaulieu, Beaulieu-sur-Mer (Alpes-Maritimes).

Mullet. Fillets with olive oil and *fleur de sel* salt, at ✳L'Algue Bleue, 62 Avenue du Général-de-Gaulle, Le Lavandou (Var, 04.94.71.05.96). From 200 to 400 F ($27–53). Fricasseed with basil at ✳Restaurant de Bacon, Antibes (Alpes-Maritimes). Served egg roll-style, at ✳Chantecler de l'Hôtel Negresco, Nice (Alpes-Maritimes).

Olive Oil. Special menu at ✳La Regalido, Rue Frédéric-Mistral, Fontvieille (Bouches-du-Rhône, 04.90.54.60.22)✳ About 160 to

400 F ($21–53). For dessert, in an emulsion accompanying strawberries and tangerine ice cream at ⚡La Bastide Saint-Antoine, Grasse (Alpes-Maritimes).

Oxtail. With orange, at ⚡La Merenda, Nice (Alpes-Maritimes).

Pistes. Mixed vegetables with basil and ribs of Swiss chard, at ⚡L'Hôtellerie Bérard, La Cadière-d'Azur (Var).

Pistou. In soup, ⚡Au Sud, Avenue des 3 Dauphins, Aiguebelle (Var, 04.94.05.76.98). From 200 to 300 F ($27–40).

Pizza. At ⚡Pizzeria Etienne, 43 Rue de Lorette, Marseille (Bouches-du-Rhône).

Porgy (pagre). In an herb crust with *pitcholine*-olive cream, at ⚡Le Vieux Colombier, Dabisse-les-Mées (Alpes-de-Haute-Provence). Baked with sautéed vegetables at ⚡La Table d'Yves, Cagnes-sur-Mer (Alpes-Maritimes).

Pot-au-feu. At ⚡L'Auberge du Clos-Sorel, village Clos-Sorel, Les Moulanès, Pra-Loup (Alpes-de-Haute-Provence, 04.92.84.10.74). From 140 to 220 F ($19–29).

Poutargue (salted and pressed fish roe). With sautéed sole, at ⚡L'Auberge de Noves, Noves (Bouches-du-Rhône). In a carpaccio of free-range veal fillets with aged Parmesan cheese, at ⚡L'Oasis, Mandelieu-La-Napoule (Alpes-Maritimes).

Prawns (crevettes). With shredded spider crab at ⚡La Bastide Saint-Antoine, Grasse (Alpes-Maritimes).

Raviolis. Homemade ravioli with borage, at ⚡Le Bel Aqua, Hôtel des Etrangers, Sospel (Alpes-Maritimes).

Risotto. With quail and white truffles at ⚡Le Nouvel Hôtel du Commerce, Castellane (Alpes-de-Haute-Provence). With summer truffles (in season) and small navy beans, at ⚡La Belle Otéro, Hôtel Carlton, Cannes (Alpes-Maritimes). With saffron and flat parsley, at ⚡Le Diamant Rose, La Colle-sur-Loup (Alpes-Maritimes). In saffron-flavored shellfish broth, at ⚡Le Chantecler, Hôtel Negresco, Nice (Alpes-Maritimes). With baby octopus in a creamy octopus-ink sauce, at ⚡L'Univers, Nice (Alpes-Maritimes). With boletus mushrooms, lamb, etc., ⚡Chez Jacques Maximin, Vence (Alpes-Maritimes).

Salad Greens. ⚡La Merenda, Nice (Alpes-Maritimes).

Sardines. Stuffed, at ⚡La Merenda, Nice (Alpes-Maritimes).

Sea Bass (bar). Raw sea bass and tiny broccoli with caviar and juniper pepper, or in fig leaves, at ⚡Bar & Bœuf, Sporting d'Eté, Monaco.

Sea-Bream (daurade). Breaded royal sea-bream, at ⚡La Terrasse de l'Hôtel Juana, Juan-les-Pins (Alpes-Maritimes).

Sea Perch (loup). In a salt crust, at ⚡L'Auberge Provençale, 61 Place Nationale, Antibes (Alpes-Maritimes, 04.93.34.13.24). From 80 to 350 F ($11–47). Loin of sea perch cooked in the skin at ⚡Métropole, Beaulieu-sur-Mer (Alpes-Maritimes). Grilled in the skin, baked, or steamed, ⚡Chez Lulou (04.93.31.00.17), Cagnes-sur-Mer (Alpes-Maritimes). Baked or in a vegetable fricassée, ⚡Aux Belles Rives, Juan-les-Pins (Alpes-Maritimes). In a crust of turmeric and violet asparagus, at ⚡Au Moulin de Mougins, Mougins (Alpes-Maritimes). In chicken broth with endive, salsify, and black truffles at ⚡Chantecler, Hôtel Negresco, Nice (Alpes-Maritimes). With fennel, spring onions, tomato dried and *taggiasche* olives, at the ⚡Louis XV-Alain Ducasse, Monaco.

Shepherd's pie. Oxtail-and-truffle shepherd's pie, at ⚡Le Fournil, Bonnieux (Vaucluse).

Spelt Bread. ⚡At the Sofitel Vieux Port, 36 Boulevard Charles Livon (04.91.15.59.00), Marseille (Bouches-du-Rhône).

Socca. With olives, at ⚡La Belle Otéro, Hôtel Carlton, Cannes (Alpes-Maritimes).

Soufflé. With tiny Morello cherries, at ⚡Villa des Lys, Hôtel Majestic, Cannes (Alpes-Maritimes).

Soup. *Au pistou* (garlic and basil), at ⚡Le Café de France, Apt (Vaucluse). Fish soup, at ⚡Restaurant de Bacon, Antibes (Alpes-Maritimes).

Squab. Roasted, at ⚡Les Santons, Place de l'Eglise, Moustiers-Sainte-Marie (Alpes-de-Haute-Provence, 04.92.74.66.48). From 220 to 380 F ($29–51). Roasted with figs, at ⚡L'Auberge de la Madone, Peillon (Alpes-Maritimes).

Squid. Stuffed, with Corsican coppa, at ⚡La Palme d'Or, Hôtel Martinez, Cannes (Alpes-Maritimes). *A la Niçoise,* at ⚡L'Univers, Nice (Alpes-Maritimes).

Stockfish (dried, unsalted fish). ⚡La Merenda, Nice (Alpes-Maritimes). In cakes, with mild garlic, at ⚡L'Univers,

Nice (Alpes-Maritimes). In *tripettes*, at ✳Le Louis XV-Alain Ducasse, Monaco.

Tapenade. In wafers, ✳Chez Jean-Jacques Jouteux, Saint-Jean-Cap-Ferrat (Alpes-Maritimes).

T-Bone Steak. Simmental beef served with large slices of fried roseval potatoes and sherry *glacée*, at ✳Bar & Bœuf, Sporting d'Eté, Monaco.

Tourtes (pies). Homemade *tourtes*, at ✳L'Auberge du Soleil, Coaraze (Alpes-Maritimes). With Swiss chard and goat cheese, at ✳Diamant Rose, La Colle-sur-Loup (Alpes-Maritimes).

Trotters. ✳Jardin d'Emile, Plage de Bestouan, Cassis (Bouches-du-Rhône, 04.42.01.80.55). ✳L'Oustau de la Foun, Château-Arnaux (Alpes-de-Haute-Provence).

Truffles. Special truffle menu in season, turbot with fondue of anchovies and truffled *beurre blanc*, at ✳L'Auberge de la Fenière, Lourmarin (Vaucluse). At ✳La Beaugravière, Mondragon (Vaucluse). ✳Chez Bruno, Lorgues (Var). At ✳Chênes Verts, Tourtour (Var). With scrambled eggs or as a garnish at ✳L'Hôtellerie de La Fuste, La Fuste (Alpes-de-Haute-Provence). White truffles at the ✳Le Louis XV-Alain Ducasse, Monaco.

Vegetables. Old-fashioned vegetables at ✳Le Clos de la Violette, Aix-en-Provence (Bouches-du-Rhône). At ✳Chênes Verts, Tourtour (Var). Sautéed, at ✳La Bastide de Moustiers, Moustiers-Sainte-Marie (Alpes-de-Haute-Provence).

Zucchini Blossoms. Fritters, at ✳L'Auberge du Jarrier, Biot (Alpes-Maritimes). ✳L'Univers, Nice (Alpes-Maritimes). ✳Chez Jacques Maximin, Vence (Alpes-Maritimes).

Tête de veau. In salad with beans, at ✳Bel Aqua, Hôtel des Etrangers, Sospel (Alpes-Maritimes).

Wine. ✳L'Ambassade des Vignobles, 42 Place Huiles, Marseille (Bouches-du-Rhône, 04.91.33.00.25). From 150 to 300 F ($20-40). ✳La Petite France, 55 Avenue de la Vallée-des-Baux, Le Paradou (Bouches-du-Rhône, 04.90.54.41.91). ✳La Beaugravière, N7, Quai du Pont Neuf, Mondragon (Vaucluse, 04.90.40.82.54). From 130 to 400 F ($17–54).

✳ Famous restaurants ✳

Villeneuve-lès-Avignon (Gard). ✳Aubertin, 1 Rue de l'Hôpital (04.90.25.94.84)✳ This restaurant with the delightful arcaded terrace, below the church, has forged a reputation for cheerful cuisine: crusty mullet and sea perch, veal cutlet braised in a hermetically sealed casserole, artichokes and boletus mushrooms Provençal style. Menus from 120 F ($16); 300 F ($40) à la carte. ✳Le Prieuré, 7 Place du Chapitre (04.90.15.90.15)✳ Here you'll find one of the loveliest gardens in Provence. Dining under the tall "platanes" is one of the most civilized rites in the region, enhanced by Serge Chenet's classic cuisine: lobster and leeks in a frothy sauce, quick-roasted fillet of john-dory with bay leaf. Remarkable wine list. Menus from 200 F ($27); 450 F ($60) à la carte.

Avignon (Vaucluse). ✳Brunel, 46 Rue de la Balance (04.90.85.24.83)✳ Stellar cuisine at reasonable prices in this restaurant just behind the Palais des Papes. Mushroom consommé with roasted foie gras, old-fashioned beef stew. Genuine Avignon cuisine. Menu 170 F ($23); 250 F ($33) à la carte. ✳Christian Etienne, 10 Rue de Mons (04.90. 86.16.50)✳ The city's up-and-coming chef features tomatoes on a special menu, plus wild sea perch cooked in its skin, roast lamb shank and *millefeuilles* of potatoes with eggplant pulp. Fine terrace directly below the Palais des Papes. Menus from 170 F ($23); 450 F ($60) à la carte. ✳La Mirande, 4 Place Amirande (04.90.85.93.93)✳ A superb residence made even better by Daniel Hébet's highly eclectic cuisine: dried beans in butter with Jabugo ham, pig's trotters stuffed with celery purée and truffles, old-fashioned French toast. Magnificent reception rooms and garden-terrace. Ask for a tour of the cellars and pantries. An incredible basement. Menus from 155 F ($21); 400 F ($53) à la carte. ✳La Vieille Fontaine, 12 Place Crillon (04.90.14. 76.76) ✳ Avignon festival goers are accustomed to gathering under the "platanes" of this superb courtyard with its burbling fountain. An institution emphasizing the classics: carpaccio of wild sea perch, fillet of pigeon with honey and spices, ivory ice cream with sweet and sour sauce. About 400 F ($53).

Gordes (Vaucluse). ✳Bastide des Cinq Lys, Chemin du Moulin, Les Beaumettes (04.90.72.38.38)✳ A fine spot, with its cypress trees and charming converted 16th-century coach inn. Regional cuisine with a modern touch under the leadership of Christophe Gillino: sautéed giant prawns and oysters, baked john-dory with caramelized orange and lemon peel, pastry shell filled with strawberries tossed in spiced wine. Menus from 180 F ($24); 400 F ($53) à la carte.

Lourmarin (Vaucluse). ✳Auberge de La Fenière, Route de Lourmarin (04.90.68.11.79)✳ In their new home, Reine and Guy Sammut offer one of the most inspired cuisines in Provence: tomato tartare and tiny violet artichokes with parmesan cheese, risotto with white truffles, braised young-rabbit dried with olive oil, fresh eggplant noodles. Menus from 200 F ($27); 450 F ($60) à la carte. ✳Le Moulin de Lourmarin, Rue du Temple (04.90.68.06.69)✳ Guy Loubet at the peak of his creative form: river pike sautéed with catmint, garden angelica, and candied grapes, rack of Sisteron lamb with wild Claparèdes thyme. Menus from 200 F ($27) ; 500 F ($67) à la carte.

Aix-en-Provence (Bouches-du-Rhône). ✳Le Clos de la Violette, 10 Avenue de la Violette, near La Villa Gallici (04.42.23.30.71)✳ An outstanding house directed by Jean-Marc Banzo, especially attractive in good weather: sea perch in a delicate ratatouille, pressed baby-mackerel and tomato dried, lamb chop and shank in herb crust. About 500 F ($67).

Les Baux (Bouches-du-Rhône). ✳La Cabro d'Or, Val d'Enfer (04.90.54.33.21)✳ A superb setting for Alain Lamaison's Provençal cuisine: potato pie with sardines and anchovies, squid stuffed with herbs in tellina broth, fillet of veal with creamy bacon sauce. Menus from 195 F ($26); 400 F ($53) à la carte. ✳L'Oustau de Baumanière, Val d'Enfer (04.90. 54.33.07)✳ Legendary Provençal cuisine served against the magnificent setting of Le Val d'Enfer, under the direction of Jean-André Charial. Crab charlotte with sautéed calamari, lightly sautéed prawns with coconut and lemon, veal kidneys in pan juices reduced with banyuls (local fortified wine). About 700 F ($93). ✳La Riboto de Taven, Val d'Enfer (04.90.54.34.23)✳ Meticulously prepared, delectable regional cuisine in an impressive setting. Baby leg of lamb with black olives and delicate fen-

nel tart, prawns *en brochette* with red rice and fillet of beef. Menus from 220 F ($29); 400 F ($53) à la carte.

Marseille (Bouches-du-Rhône). ✳Le Petit Nice, Maldormé bend on the Corniche Kennedy (04.91.59.25.92)✳ A vivid classic in a sumptuous setting facing the Mediterranean. Lobster pie with sauce *bressane*, porgy with caviar and citronella, fillets of rock mullet with pistachio cream. Menus from 500 F ($67); 750 F ($100) à la carte.

Noves (Bouches-du-Rhône). ✳Auberge de Noves, on D28 between Noves and Château-Renard (04.90.24.28.28)✳ In a typical, restored, *bastide* overlooking Provence, a renowned classic with a modern slant: snail soufflé with pine nuts and mild garlic, large sautéed sole with pressed fish-roe butter, rack of lamb with rosemary-flavored pan juices. Menus from 230 F ($31); 500 F ($67) à la carte.

Callas (Var). ✳Hostellerie des Gorges de Pennafort, quartier Pennafort (04.94.76.66.51)✳ The work of gifted chef Philippe da Silva (formerly of Chiberta in Paris), emphasizing fresh market produce served in a vast house set against an unspoiled landscape. Fricassee of snails and pig trotters with marjoram, roast rack of lamb with tarragon-flavored pan juices, pastry shell with pears and Fourme d'Ambert blue cheese. Menus from 265 F ($35); 350 F ($47) à la carte.

Gassin (Var). ✳Villa Belrose, Boulevard des Crêtes (04.94.55.97.97)✳ With a fine view over the Bay of Saint-Tropez, Thierry Thiercelin's cuisine has a fitting backdrop. Grilled fillet of sea perch in its skin, crusty spelt risotto with aged parmesan cheese and parsley essence, honey cake with pecans and grapefruit. Menus from 250 F ($33); 500 F ($67) à la carte. ✳Mas de Tourteron, Les Imberts (04.90.72.00.16)✳ At this converted 18th-century silkworm-breeding farm, Elisabeth Bourgeois concocts a subtle and inspired cuisine. *Bohémienne* of vegetables and dried-bean salad with *pistou*, marinade of sea and river fish with borage fritters, green-tomato dried and custard with golden glints of cardamine. Menus from 160 F ($21); 300 F ($40) à la carte.

Grimaud (Var). ✳Les Santons, in the village, on the main highway (04.94.43.21.02)✳ This cult restaurant of the 1970s is still going strong. Maître Cuisinier de France Claude Girard offers young rabbit stuffed with olives, roast Gandels squab with mild spices and Provençal honey, creamy lobster risotto. Menus from 215 F ($29); 500 F ($67) à la carte.

Lorgues (Var). ✳Chez Bruno, Route de Vidauban (04.94.85.93.93)✳ The truffle emperor, here reigning over a powerful gastronomic kingdom in a magical setting. One of the best restaurants on the coast, with a basic menu at 300 F ($40) featuring salad with walnut oil, braised vegetables with country bacon and crawfish, scalloped potatoes, creamed white and Italian truffles, pigeon in flaky pastry with foie gras and truffles, strawberry soup with spiced wine.

Saint-Tropez (Var). ✳La Bastide de Saint-Tropez, Route des Carles (04.94.97.58.16)✳ A restaurant renowned in the area for its regional cuisine. John-dory baked with aromatic eggplant butter and tiny braised white onions, roast pigeon with a creamy truffled spelt risotto and *brochette* of giblets. Menus from 220 F ($29); 500 F ($67) à la carte. ✳Résidence de la Pinède, Plage de la Bouillabaisse (04.94.55.91.00)✳ A restaurant with a heavenly location on the banks of the gulf and an open kitchen for stimulating appetites. Risotto with aged-parmesan cheese wafers, cannelloni stuffed with ricotta and San Daniele, fresh-cheese fritters with herbs, slivers of fresh cod poached in fennel broth. Menus from 300 F ($40); 700 F ($93) à la carte. ✳Maison Leï Mouscardins, Rue Portalet (04.94.97.29.00)✳ A view that's a treat in itself, with the added attraction of Laurent Tarridec's vibrant cuisine. Baked fillet of sea perch studded with szechwan peppercorns, crawfish sautéed with crushed chestnuts, truffles and morels. Menus from 330 F ($44); 700 F ($93) à la carte.

Tourtour (Var). ✳Les Chênes Verts, Route de Villecroze (04.94.70.55.06)✳ An old-fashioned restaurant with a classic repertoire, especially in winter with its fine truffle selections. Also in season, green asparagus with cream of morels, quail in pastry, spelt risotto and roast free-range pigeon with mild garlic. Menus from 250 F ($33); 500 F ($67) à la carte.

Château-Arnoux (Alpes-de-Haute-Provence). ✳️ La Bonne Etape, Chemin du Lac (04.92.64.00.09) ✳️ One of Provence's great restaurants, in a restored 18th-century coach inn surrounded by olive groves and directed by Jany Gleize. Boletus-and-morel pastry with white truffles, loin of rabbit with hyssop, and fresh pasta with lemon. Menus from 225 F ($30); 400 F ($53) à la carte. ✳️ L'Oustaou de la Foun, on N85 direction Sisteron, a little over a mile from Château-Arnoux (04.92.62.65.30) ✳️ A new and continuously evolving star in the regional-cuisine firmament (Gérald Jourdan, chef). Charcoal-grilled fillet of fresh red tuna, spicy ratatouille and potato ravioli, sautéed veal, cream of bitter almonds in sugar-cured tomatoes. Menus from 120 F ($16); 300 F ($40) à la carte.

La Fuste (Alpes-de-Haute-Provence). ✳️ Hôtellerie de La Fuste, Route d'Oraison (04.92.72.05.95) ✳️ Peerless yet practical classicism at Daniel Jourdan's *bastide*. Truffles in scrambled eggs, local shoulder of lamb, pastry with wild-strawberry sauce. Menus from 250 F ($33); 500 F ($67) à la carte.

Antibes (Alpes-Maritimes). ✳️ Restaurant de Bacon, Cap d'Antibes (04.93.61.50.02) ✳️ A palace of fish run by Adrien and Etienne Sordello, who respect a family tradition inaugurated in 1948. Sea perch with olives, aioli with baby vegetables, *rouille*, bouillabaisse. When you add to that a marvelous view overlooking the ramparts of Old Antibes and a splendid wine list, you know you're in the right place. Menus from 250 F ($33); 500 F ($67) à la carte. ✳️ La Bonne Auberge, Philippe Rostang, on N 7, between La Brague and Le Parc de Vaugrenier (04.93.33.36.65) ✳️ A revered classic enlivened by touches of modernity: stuffed marrow bones *au pot-au-feu*, thin fillet of sea perch in soy butter. 200 F ($27) à la carte.

Beaulieu-sur-Mer (Alpes-Maritimes). ✳️ Le Métropole, 15 Boulevard du Maréchal Leclerc (04.93.01.00.08) ✳️ A traditional restaurant in which Christian Métral offers his inventions on a garden-terrace overlooking the Mediterranean and Cap-Ferrat. Hen-pheasant consommé with chestnuts and truffles, prawn ravioli with artichokes, loin of sea perch cooked in its skin. Menus from 300 F ($40); 600 F ($80) à la carte. ✳️ La Réserve de Beaulieu, 5 Boulevard du Général Leclerc (04.93.01.28.99) ✳️ A famous restaurant infused with fresh life by Jean-Claude Delion (of La Pinède, Saint-Tropez). In the kitchen, Christophe Cussac concocts dishes boasting a sunny discipline: giant prawns and *bohémienne* of vegetables *al dente* in sweet and sour Campari sauce, john-dory minestrone with chilled basil and tapenade wafers. Menus from 300 F ($40); 800 F ($107) à la carte.

Biot (Alpes-Maritimes). ✳️ Auberge du Jarrier, Passage de la Bourgade (04.93.65.11.68) ✳️ Christian Métral has moved to La Réserve de Beaulieu, but his wife carries on the culinary tradition of this Provençal inn. Fricassee of lamb sweetbreads and lambs-lettuce salad, loin of sea-bream grilled in its skin, blueberry pastry. Menus from 310 F ($41); 400 F ($53) à la carte.

Cannes (Alpes-Maritimes). ✳️ La Belle Otéro, Hôtel Carlton, La Croisette (04.92.99.51.10) ✳️ For Francis Chauveau's delightfully Mediterranean cuisine, concocted at his perch on the seventh floor. Morel lasagna with violet Provençal asparagus and crisp prawns, john-dory with spiny artichokes, spring navy beans, and Jabugo ham. Menus from 290 F ($39); 600 F ($80) à la carte. ✳️ La Palme d'Or, Hôtel Martinez, La Croisette (04.92.98.74.14) ✳️ Classically rigorous Christian Willer produces his Mediterranean repertoire in an Art Deco setting. Creamy green peas with savory, braised prawns with morels, fricassée of morels and violet asparagus, potato gnocchi dusted with parmesan cheese, fillet of mullet sautéed with braised calamari, small white beans with curry and celery leaves. Menus from 450 F ($60); 600 F ($80) à la carte. ✳️ Villa des Lys, Le Majestic, la Croisette (04.92.98.77.00) ✳️ A well deserved success for Bruno Oger (trained with Georges Blanc), who moves with agility between regional cuisine and high classicism. Giant roasted prawns with bouillabaisse risotto, brill braised in a sealed casserole, young lacquered rabbit with pimento-and-eggplant dried. Menus from 260 F ($35); 550 F ($73) à la carte.

La Colle-sur-Loup (Alpes-Maritimes). ✳️ Le Diamant Rose, Route de Saint-Paul (04.93.32.82.20) ✳️ Generous traditional cuisine based on fresh market produce and served in an authentic Provençal villa. Daniel Ettlinger offers local violet asparagus with fresh tomatoes or risotto *piemontese* with roast quail and green peas. Menus from 240 F ($32); 600 F ($80) à la carte.

Eze-Village (Alpes-Maritimes). ⊁Château de la Chèvre d'Or, Rue du Barri (04.92.10.66.66)⊁ A great classic spectacularly perched above a vast landscape, this year boasting a new chef: Jean-Marc Delacourt. Among his concoctions: grilled giant prawns accompanied by summer squash and lemon butter flavored with Espelette pimento, braised medallion of turbot with slices of potato and country bacon, fillet of lamb stuffed with tomatoes and garlic dried. Menus from 280 F ($37); 700 F ($93) à la carte. ⊁Château Eza, Rue Pise⊁ Once the residence of William of Sweden, a dazzling view and classic cuisine: sautéed green asparagus with boletus and morel mushrooms, rack of lamb au gratin with ratatouille *à la Niçoise*. Menus from 350 F ($47); 600 F ($80) à la carte.

Grasse (Alpes-Maritimes). ⊁Jacques Chibois, La Bastide Saint-Antoine, 48 Avenue Henri Dunant (04.93.70.94.94) ⊁ Veal kidneys with shredded violet artichoke and polenta, fan of mullet on salad of local vegetables, parsley, and olive oil. Menus from 490 F ($35); 700 F ($93) à la carte.

Juan-les-Pins (Alpes-Maritimes). ⊁Les Belles Rives, Boulevard du Littoral (04.93.61.02.79)⊁ An amazing relic of the 1930s (Scott Fitzgerald once stayed here), with a stylish cuisine that's right up-to-date: prawn fritters with Thai spices, john-dory fillet cooked in its skin, farm-raised veal cutlet *en casserole*. Menus from 190 F ($25); 450 F ($60) à la carte. ⊁La Terrasse, Hôtel Juana, La Pinède, Avenue Gallice (04.93.61.20.37)⊁ A coastal cult restaurant today directed by Christian Morisset with discipline and energy. Zucchini spaghetti with butter and *cromesqui*-style tomato ramekins, saddle of Pauillac lamb cooked in the rose-colored clay of Vallauris, Menton-lemon soufflé pie and strawberry sherbet. Menus from 490 F ($65); 800 F ($107) à la carte.

Mandelieu-La-Napoule (Alpes-Maritimes). ⊁L'Oasis, Rue Jean Honoré Carle (04.93.49.95.52)⊁ Mastery with a Mediterranean touch for Stéphane Raimbault's cuisine, in an exuberant Riviera setting. Prawns *marinière*, cuttlefish-ink ravioli, saffron risotto in a golden crust, warm foie gras on a bed of Swiss chard. Menus from 320 F ($43); 650 F ($87) à la carte.

Mougins (Alpes-Maritimes). ⊁La Ferme de Mougins, 10 Avenue Saint Basile (04.93.90.03.74)⊁ A warm welcome from Henri Sauvanet, lush garden, exquisite terrace. Fillet of john-dory with rosemary oil, free-range pigeon in pan juices *à la Provençale* and herb ravioli. Menus from 250 F ($33); 450 F ($60) à la carte. ⊁Le Moulin de Mougins, Quartier Notre Dame de Vie (04.93.75.78.24)⊁ Roger Vergé respects and perpetuates the tradition of fine Mediterranean cuisine: rock mullet and tellinas with saffron and lemon dried accented of vegetables *à l'orientale*, roast-chicken *ballottine* stuffed with a *matignon* of vegetables and served with a fricassee of asparagus and chanterelles mushrooms, Port wine sauce. Menus from 250 F ($33); 1 000 F ($133) à la carte.

Nice (Alpes-Maritimes). ⊁Le Chantecler, Hôtel Negresco, Promenade des Anglais (04.93.16.64.00)⊁ A legendary institution that continues its brilliant interpretations of regional cuisine under the disciplined hand of Alain Llorca. Foie gras and tapas, egg rolls and lobster, roast pigeon with apricots, tomato timbale, ice cream with olive dried, herb pie and sautéed asparagus. Menus from 430 F ($57); 600 F ($80) à la carte. ⊁La Merenda, 4 Rue de la Terrasse (no telephone)⊁ Dominique Le Stanc's unpretentious and inspired cuisine in a tiny, absolutely authentic Nice bistro. Stuffed sardines, zucchini fritters, fresh pasta with *pistou*, tripe *à la Niçoise*, stockfish (dried fish), oxtail *à l'orange*. About 200 F ($27). ⊁L'Univers, 54 Boulevard Jean Jaurès (04.93.62.32.22)⊁ Distinctive regional cuisine by Christian Plumail served near the city's main boulevards. Violet-artichoke salad with parmesan cheese and arugula, stuffed squid *à la Niçoise* and zucchini fritters, rabbit *en casserole*, dried-cod wafer with mild garlic. Menus from 100 F ($13); 350 F ($47) à la carte.

Roquebrune-Cap-Martin (Alpes-Maritimes). ⊁Le Roquebrune, 100, Corniche Inférieure (04.93.35.00.16)⊁ The Marinovich sisters emphasize the sea and typical Côte d'Azur recipes, using fish caught the same day (poached, grilled, meu-

nière), bouillabaisse, lobster, and crayfish—plus Parma ham and Brigue leg of lamb. Menus from 230 F ($31); 700 F ($93) à la carte. ✳Le Vistaero, Grande Corniche (04.92.10.40.20)✳ A breathtaking view, and Jean-Pierre Pestre's meticulous cuisine: large boletus-mushroom ravioli with anise and spinach, crusty scampi fritters and eggplant with basil and sweet and sour tomatoes, fillet of john-dory grilled with saffron-flavored carrot purée. Menus from 190 F ($25); 600 F ($80) à la carte.

Saint-Jean-Cap-Ferrat (Alpes-Maritimes). ✳Jean-Jacques Jouteux, 2 Avenue Denis Séméria (04.93.76.03.97)✳ A culinary genius exercising his talents to the full: large ravioli with quick-cooked ratatouille, potato *millefeuilles* and giant prawns with hazelnut butter and shellfish broth, baked john-dory with calamari and violet artichokes, saddle of lamb in spice crust and potatoes au gratin. Menus from 250 F ($33); 600 F ($80) à la carte. ✳Grand Hôtel du Cap, Le Cap, Boulevard du Général de Gaulle (04.93.76.50.50)✳ A lovely Riviera villa with cuisine to match: marinade of baby mackerel with herbs and mixed greens, prawn soup with *pistou*, fillets of rock mullet with *brandade* and *chiffonade* of fresh tomatoes with basil oil. Menus from 270 F ($36); 700 F ($93) à la carte. ✳La Voile d'Or, Port de Plaisance (04.93.01.13.13)✳ A lovely Riviera villa with cuisine to match: marinade of baby mackerel with herbs and mixed greens, prawn soup with *pistou*, filet of rock mullet with *brandade* and chiffonade of fresh tomatoes with basil oil. Menus from 270 F ($36); 750 F ($100) à la carte.

Saint-Martin-du-Var (Alpes-Maritimes). ✳Issautier, Route de Digne, N 202 (04.93.08.10.65)✳ A great restaurant specializing in regional Provençal dishes and inspired by Jean-François Issauter. Gattières zucchini with its mushroom-stuffed blossoms, veal kidney roasted whole with red-onion dried and Bandol wine, rump of Sisteron lamb cooked rare with fresh mint and local navy beans, blueberry pie in a sweet crust, tangerines au gratin (crème-brûlée style). Menus from 270 F ($36); 600 F ($80) à la carte.

Vence (Alpes-Maritimes). ✳Jacques Maximin, 689 Chemin de la Gaude (04.93.58.90.75)✳ One of the greatest chefs of our time, in a villa glowing with flowers and freshness. Vinaigrette of clams and shredded cuttlefish with spring onions, fresh rolled anchovies and sautéed scallops, fillet of squab with fresh morels. Menus from 240 F ($32); 500 F ($67) à la carte.

Monaco. ✳Le Louis XV-Alain Ducasse, place du Casino (00.377.92.16.30.01)✳ The Riviera at its very best. Restaurant directed by my assistant, Franck Cerutti. Squab from La Motte-du-Caire in Haute-Provence with aromatic pan juices; grilled *gamberoni* from the Gulf of Genoa with bitter endive and pressed fish roe from Martigues; gnocchi made with mona lisa potatoes and white truffles from Alba (in season); loin of Beauce rabbit *en brochette* with red-wine sauce accompanied by roast pumpkin, beets, celery, and boletus mushrooms. Menus from 500 F ($67); 1,000 F ($133) à la carte.

✳ Good small restaurants ✳

Aigues-Mortes (Gard). ✳Los Caracolès, Mas des marais, Route du Bosquet (04.66.53.71.98)✳ A charming Provençal *mas*, with Spanish-style courtyard and large dining room—the perfect place for carefree summer dining. This table d'hôte located on the windblown Camargue exemplifies pure simplicity. Products from land and sea are purchased daily for dishes such as sardine fritters, mussels and prawns, salt cod, stuffed eggplant, grilled beef, and grilled sea perch with fennel.

Apt (Vaucluse). ✳Café de France, Place de la Bouquerie (04.90.74.22.01)✳ Being located opposite an open market can make things a little noisy, and few markets are noisier than the one in Apt, with its vivid sights and sounds, its characteristic verve and energy. The servers here respond with admirable finesse, offering various soothing remedies (green salad with Banon goat cheese, *pistou* soup, timbale of dried cod with leeks, Provençal-style artichokes) to soothe the spirit. When you add a few bravura numbers (calf's-head *ravigote*, stuffed tomatoes), total peace reigns. About 150 F ($20).

Bonnieux (Vaucluse). Le Fournil, 5 Place Carnot (04.90.75.83.62). An excellent restaurant featuring regional cuisine: tartare of eggplant dried with fresh marinated anchovies, oxtail-and-truffle shepherd's pie. About 200 F ($27).

Mondragon (Vaucluse). ✳La Beaugravière, N7, Quai du Pont Neuf (04.90.40.82.54)✳ Guy Jullien's regional cuisine, focused (in season) on truffles and backed up by one of the finest selections of Côtes-du-Rhône in the world. From 140 to 400 F ($19–53).

Pernes-les-Fontaines (Vaucluse). ✳Au Fil du Temps, Place Louis Giraud (04.90.66.48.61)✳ The 195 F menu ($26) boasts a succession of hearty dishes including quail pâté with onion dried, burbot with tarragon, and raspberry tart. The cuisine at the Fil du Temps seems to reflect its own name, recognizing that time goes by too fast and could leave this little Provençal square behind, languishing in twilit lethargy.

Marseille (Bouches-du-Rhône). ✳L'Epuisette, Vallon des Auffes (04.91.52.17.82)✳ At the seaside, Jean-Michel Besnard's regional cuisine, including his famous baby-vegetable pie. About 250 F ($33).

Saint-Rémy-de-Provence (Bouches-du-Rhône). ✳La Maison Jaune, 15 Rue Carnot (04.90.92.56.14)✳ Although in this land of "Provençal chic" a certain understated elegance has long been the rule, offering a 120 F menu ($16), involves stripping all the way down to bare essentials—which makes cheating difficult. This unpretentious cuisine in soft ochers and pastels at first holds back, and then hums a little tune, as you might do on a train to while away the time. Marinated salmon the size of a CD, roast chicken with lemon-flavored oil, citrus soup. About 200 F ($27).

La Cadière-d'Azur (Var). ✳Hôtellerie Bérard, Rue Gabriel Péri (04.94.90.11.43)✳ The dining experience at Danièle and René Bérard's is the result of a truly great restaurant opting for simplicity. A consummate example of genuine Provençal cuisine. About 350 F ($47).

Castellane (Alpes-de-Haute-Provence). ✳Le Nouvel Hôtel du Commerce, Place de l'Eglise (04.92.83.61.00)✳ Inspired cuisine produced by one of my former pupils, a display of regional dishes at their very best. From 120 to 350 F ($16–47).

Dabisse-les-Mées (Alpes-de-Haute-Provence). ✳Le Vieux Colombier, D 4, La Bastide Blanche (04.92.34.32.32)✳ Opposite the Lurs hills, in a slightly out-of-the-way location, the extremely talented Sylvain Nowak offers a cuisine including baked fillet of sea perch with artichokes Provençal-style, porgy in herb crust. About 300 F ($40).

Moustiers-Sainte-Marie (Alpes-de-Haute-Provence). ✳La Bastide de Moustiers, Quartier Saint Michel, Chemin de Quinson (04.92.70.47.47)✳ A serene, peaceful take on Provence, deploying its charm through airy, uncomplicated dishes served in exquisite surroundings. Eggplant-purée canapé and cucumber tartare, sautéed vegetables, spit-roasted sucking pig, country-veal cutlet with black truffles. One of the most brilliant successes of recent years. About 300 F ($40).

Cagnes-sur-Mer (Alpes-Maritimes). ✳La Table d'Yves, 85 Montée de la Bourgade (04.93.20.33.33)✳ A chef formerly at the Royal Riviera in Saint-Jean-Cap-Ferrat, who now directs this charming little restaurant offering relaxed cuisine: baked porgy and sautéed vegetables, ricotta ravioli. About 200 F ($27).

Coaraze (Alpes-Maritimes). ✹ Auberge du Soleil, Vieux Village (04.93.79.08.11) ✹ An exquisite village, a sense of time past and delectably simple cuisine. Homemade main-dish pies, rabbit fricassée. About 200 F ($27).

Nice (Alpes-Maritimes). ✹ La Zucca Magica, 4-bis Quai Papacino (04.93.56.25.27) ✹ The moment you arrive here you'll be offered a vegetable-parmesan timbale, as if to assuage your barbarian ardor. Next comes a succession of appetizers that are meals in themselves: lasagna with pesto, pasta with lentils, tagliatelli with vegetables, rigatoni, borzotti with squash and walnuts, sage-and-potato pie. Lunch (only) menu for 80 F ($11), à la carte about 150 F ($20).

Peillon (Alpes-Maritimes). ✹ Auberge de la Madone, Place Auguste Arnulf (04.93.79.91.17) ✹ A traditional emphasis in a delightful village setting, cuisine reflecting the Nice region: zucchini fritters, rack of lamb, young rabbit in aspic with mixed dried fruits and nuts. About 250 F ($33).

Saint-Paul-de-Vence (Alpes-Maritimes). ✹ La Colombe d'Or, Place du Général de Gaulle (04.93.32.80.02) ✹ You could once have dined with Picasso, Modigliani, Matisse, or Bonnard in this lovely patio mysteriously unaffected by shifts in fashion. Mediterranean cuisine. About 450 F ($64).

Sospel (Alpes-Maritimes). ✹ Le Bel Aqua, Hôtel des Etrangers, Boulevard de Verdun (04.93.04.00.09) ✹ Gilles Domerego has caused a sensation with his enlightened regional cooking and modest prices. Homemade borage ravioli, roasted free-range guinea hen with rosemary en *casserole*, stuffed loin of young rabbit, fricasséed fillets and legs of quail with hyssop, green peas, and artichokes, Carros strawberry pie in a tender sweet crust, authentic Florentine tiramisù. About 200 F ($27).

Monaco. ✹ Bar & Bœuf, Sporting d'Eté, Avenue Princesse Grace (00.377.92.16.60.60) ✹ One of the coast's trendiest spots, offering a host a fresh ideas: raw sea bass with tiny broccoli and caviar, fillet of sea bass in fig leaves, Simmental T-bone steak with large slices of fried Roseval potatoes and sherry ice. About 500 F ($67).

Recommended reading: ✹ *Guide Gantié de la Provence* ✹ A remarkable guide to Provence and the Côte d'Azur published annually by Jacques Gantié, listing 800 fine restaurants and 450 gourmet products. Informed, knowledgeable, practical.

* * *

ACCOMMODATIONS

When I see a place that appeals to me, I always want
to spend the night there. This is the time for bonding. I feel
as though I were becoming part of the land, the warp-and-woof
of the region, the fragrances in its air. What I like to do in
Provence is to wander at leisure and then, at nightfall, to look
for an inn — a home-away-from-home — where I can dine, sleep, and
wake up again in the morning. Whether in a luxury hotel or unpretentious farmhouse, the room itself is part of the pleasure. I
spend my life in hotel rooms, but in Provence I feel at home
everywhere. The region's restaurants and guest rooms are promonto-
ries from which to savor the magic of the moment. I use the
opportunity to stand back from things a little, to get in touch
with myself. I can also use the room for an afternoon nap,
something that in my view is the ultimate in the luxurious art
of living. Siesta time brings with it irrefutable proof of a body
at ease, relaxed, rested. I appreciate these moments stolen from
an active, practical life.

I love doing nothing, letting time slip by, watching the shadows
move across the ceiling. I then have a genuine feeling of belonging
to the world, my bed at it center, the cosmos revolving around it.

• • •

View from a room at La Colombe d'Or ⟶

156

✳ Recommended accommodations ✳ www.chateauxhotels.com

Bonnieux (Vaucluse). ✳Clos du Buis, Rue Victor Hugo, Philippe Paurin (04.90.75.88.48)✳ Six charming Provençal-style rooms with beamed ceilings, from 400 F ($53). Swimming pool. ✳Mas des Trois Sources, Caroline Guinard and Paul Jeannet (04.90.75.95.58)✳ Opposite the Lubéron, between Bonnieux and the Château de Sade, at Lacoste, five vast rooms from 400 F ($53).

Cabrières-d'Avignon (Vaucluse). ✳Bastide de Voulonne, Quartier Voulonne (04.90.76.77.56)✳ A traditional 18th-century Provençal *bastide* with a superb restaurant, nestled in a 12-acre garden. Swimming pool. A total of five rooms, from 600 F ($80).

Goult (Vaucluse). ✳La Médecine, La Bégude (04.90.72.49.50)✳ A secular residence on the Calavan plain at the foot of the mountain, with five pleasantly furnished rooms from 600 F ($80). Swimming pool.

Lourmarin (Vaucluse). ✳Hôtel de Guilles, Route des Vaugines (04.90.68.30.55)✳ A traditional *bastide* set amid vineyards and a grove of almond, olive, and cherry trees. Its hushed quiet and excellent restaurant make this a desirable stop. Rooms from 400 F ($53). Tennis, swimming pool. Also, ✳La Fenière, Route de Cadenet (04.90.68.11.79)✳ Reine and Guy Sammut's world, set amid a stunning landscape. Rooms from 500 to 950 F ($67–217). And, lastly, ✳Le Moulin de Lourmarin (04.90.68.06.69)✳ An extremely comfortable hotel located in the center of the village, opposite the castle. Rooms from 600 to 1,300 F ($80–173).

Oppède (Vaucluse). ✳Le Mourre, Victorine Canac (04.90.76.99.31)✳ Four cottages sleeping two to six (rates vary depending on the season; reserve at least six months in advance). A large, cheerful *mas* with blue shutters, an old dovecote, a tenant house, and an old mill rented by the week. Swimming pool.

Roussillon (Vaucluse). ✳Mamaison, Quartier Les Devens (04.90.05.74.17 – mamaison@provence.com)✳ This old 18th-century farmhouse between Bonnieux and Lacoste has been restored with taste and a respect for the past, creating a peaceful, friendly atmosphere. Rooms from 450 to 850 F ($60–113). The menu has a vegetarian slant and emphasizes seafood.

Saint-Saturnin-les-Apt (Vaucluse). ✳Maison Garance, Hameau des Bassacs (04.90.05.74.61)✳ Adjacent to Gordes, six rooms (with an orange grove planned for the future) in the center of this "watercolorists' hamlet." From 600 to 750 F ($80–100). Calm, peaceful. *Table d'hôte* restaurant for guests.

Arles (Bouches-du-Rhône). ✳Le Nord Pinus, 6 Rue du Palais (04.90.93.44.44)✳ A residence restored with reverence and talent in 1989 by Agnès Guigou around a "corrida" theme. The style shifts to white-and-gray on the fourth floor, boasting 2 particularly attractive rooms: No. 30 (with penthouse terrace) and No. 34. Also available: six apartments renting for 1,700 F ($227), and 24 rooms from 770 to 1,700 F ($103–227). ✳Le Mas de Peint, Le Sambuc (04.90.97.20.62)✳ On a 1,000-acre estate, a traditional 18th-century *mas* with eight rooms and three suites renting for 1,195 to 2,180 F ($159–291). Comfortable furnishings, swimming pool, bridle paths, and a fine restaurant serving meals for about 250 F ($33).

Les Baux-de-Provence (Bouches-du-Rhône). ✳L'Oustau de Baumanières, Chemin Départemental No. 27 (04.90.54.33.07)✳ Not only luxurious Provençal-style rooms, but also delightful separate cottages, in an atmosphere of peace and calm. From 1,500 to 1,850 F ($200–247).

Maussan-les-Alpilles (Bouches-du-Rhône). ✳Le Mas des Olivades, Quartier Bourgeac, Chemin Mérigot (04.90.54.56.78)✳ Set in an olive grove adjacent to the village, at the foot of Les Baux-de-Provence, a traditional *mas* in a natural setting. Double rooms from 690 F ($92). Swimming pool, *table d'hôte* restaurant for guests.

Saint-Rémy-de-Provence (Bouches-du-Rhône). ✳Le Mas de l'Ange, Petite Route de Saint-Rémy-de-Provence, 13940 Mollèges (04.90.95.08.33)✳ Near the foothills of the Alps, six quiet and attractive rooms for 400 F ($53).

Bargème (Var). ✳Les Roses Trémières, Place du Village (04.94.84.20.86)✳ In one of the loveliest villages of France, a few guest rooms surrounded by shady pathways, ancient stones, and fortified gates.

La Cadière-d'Azur (Var). ✳Hostellerie Berard, 6 Rue Gabriel Péri (04.94.90.11.43)✳ Pagnol's Provence, in the center of a lively village. Ideally located (near Toulon and Marseille), this for-

mer 11th-century convent maintains a warm simplicity despite its renown. Rooms from 510 to 1,200 F ($68–160) and an excellent restaurant (from 160 to 295 F – $21–39).

La Celle (Var). ✳ Hostellerie de l'Abbaye de la Celle, Place du Général de Gaulle (04.98.05.14.14 – contact@abbaye-celle. com) ✳ In the Var back country, a superb architectural ensemble (fine 12th-century chapter house) overlooking the village. A dozen or so rooms decorated in luxurious simplicity. From 1,300 to 1,900 F ($173–253). Garden, swimming pool, golf course nearby. Meals from 200 to 350 F ($27–47).

Fayence (Var). ✳ Le Moulin de la Camandoule, Chemin rural Notre Dame des Cyprès (04.94.76.00.84) ✳ A former olive-oil mill on the banks of the Camandre River, run by an English couple. Some 10 rooms decorated Provençal-style for a restful and delightful stay. From 500 F ($67) per person, demi-pension.

Lorgues (Var). ✳ Chez Bruno, 2350 Route des Arcs (04.94. 85.93.93) ✳ The emperor of the truffle has extended his renowned restaurant with its delectable cuisine to include a few rooms decorated in typical Provençal style. From 500 F ($67).

Seillans (Var). ✳ Hôtel des Deux Rocs, Place Font d'Amont 04.94.76.87.32) ✳ A fine 18th-century Provençal residence perched against the ramparts of the old château, on a little square where visitors can enjoy breakfast in warm weather. Attractive rooms and a warm welcome. Double rooms from 420 F ($56).

Trigance (Var). ✳ Le Château de Trigance, Montée Saint Roch (04.94.76.91.18) ✳ A noble and historic residence atop its own mountain peak. Baggage is drawn up by pulley (a sight that brings a sentimental tear to the eye). Double rooms from 600 F ($80).

Moustiers-Sainte-Marie (Alpes-de-Haute-Provence). ✳ La Bastide de Moustiers, Quartier Saint Michel (04.92.70. 47.47 – labastide@alain-ducasse.com) ✳ This estate, once owned by a 17th-century master ceramist, reinvents old-fashioned charm with a professionalism that's consummate without being obvious. The establishment's 12 rooms include La Volière (sunny and yellow), La Blanche (a kind of nubile cocoon with a vast bathroom), La Framboise, and La Lavande. Double-rooms from 900 to 1,520 F ($120–203).

Coaraze (Alpes-Maritimes). ✳ L'Auberge du Soleil, Place du Village (04.93.79.08.11) ✳ A warm, simple, authentic setting. Rustic rooms with impressive views, a family-pension atmosphere marked by respectful courtesy and unobtrusive service. To top it off, a restaurant in the same vein (from 150 to 280 F – $20–37) offering deliciously simple fare. Swimming pool. Rooms from 330 F ($44).

Juan-les-Pins (Alpes-Maritimes). ✳ Les Belles Rives, Boulevard du Littoral (04.93.61.02.79) ✳ The rooms on the wings and those with a sea view (Nos. 63, 79, and 95) are the best, of course; but No. 66 is recommended for a single occupant, and No. 50 for its delightful terrace. This is no vast, modern palace, but an exquisite and friendly pension with an Art Deco slant. Double rooms from 1,250 F ($167).

Nice (Alpes-Maritimes). ✳ Hôtel Windsor, 11 Rue Dalpozzo (04.93.88.59.35) ✳ A step away from the Promenade des Anglais, this hotel has succeeded in adding modern touches (rooms designed by artists) and boasts a tropical garden filled with unusual birds and plants. Swimming pool. Rooms from 550 to 700 F ($73–93).

Saint-Paul-de-Vence (Alpes-Maritimes). ✳ La Colombe d'Or, Place du Général de Gaulle (04.93.32.80.02) ✳ With true Mediterranean volubility—as though safeguarding its storied past—the eight-volume guest book is filled with endless riches. In the off season, La Colombe d'Or is definitely one of the most civilized spots in Europe. And, by great good chance, perfect comfort is also part of the mix. A total of 16 beautiful rooms, from 1,300 F ($173). The best is No. 24, with its splendid view of Saint-Paul-de-Vence.

Monaco. ✳ Hôtel de Paris, Place du Casino (00.377.92.16. 30.00) ✳ One of the few remaining palaces on the Côte d'Azur, with 154 rooms and 43 apartments. Magnificent. From 2,000 to 4,920 F ($267–656). ✳ Monte-Carlo Beach Hotel, Avenue Princesse Grace (00.377.93.30.98.80) ✳ Fans of Helmut Newton's style should know that the famed photographer had his "natural" studio here. If the Riviera represents anything, it's this kind of artificial yet appealing paradise. Some prefer the rooms on the beach (Nos. 21, 41, 51, 61, and 62); others like to be near the rocks (Nos. 33, 50, 60, 72). Forty-five rooms from 2,400 to 2,700 F ($320–360), suites from 1,745 to 5,500 F ($233–733).

DRôME

Nyons

GARD

Bollène

VAUCLUSE

Crillon-le-Brave

Villeneuve-lès-Avignon

Carpentras

Rhône

Avignon

Apt

St-Etienne-Les-Orgues

Les Mées

Barrême

ALPES-DE-HAUTE-PROVENCE

St-André-les-Alpes

Fontan

Saorge

Château-Renard

Cavaillon

Forcalquier

Valensole

Castellane

ALPES-MARITIMES

Graveson

Durance

Lourmarin

Moustiers-Ste-Marie

La Palud-sur-Verdon

Apremont

St-Rémy-de-Provence

Arles

Aigues-Mortes

Salon-de-Provence

La Bastide

Gourdon

St-Paul-de-Vence

Menton

Monaco

Le sambuc

BOUCHES-DU-RHône

Bargème

Grasse

Biot

Eze

La Gaude

La Camargue

Aix-en-Provencè

VAR

Callas

Nice

Vence

Stes-Maries-de-la-Mer

Gardanne

Cannes

Tourettes-sur-Loup

Martigues

Aubagnè

Forcalqueiret

Lorgues

Roquefort-les-Pins

Les Baux-de-Provence

Le Paradou

Marseille

Cassis

La Cadière-d'Azur

Grimaud

St-Tropez

Eyguières

Le Puy-Ste-Réparade

Mediterranean Sea

15 miles

• Photo and illustration credits

✳ Prosper Assouline/Editions Assouline: pages 43 (Colombe d'Or), 47, 103, 127 (Colombe d'Or), 129, 149 (Colombe d'Or), 151, 155, 157.

✳ Georges Braque/Adagp, Paris 2000: pages 79, 93.

✳ Colombe d'Or/Roux: pages 72 (top), 117.

✳ *Cuisine et Vins de France*/All rights reserved: pages 133, 134 (market stall), 136.

✳ Alain Ducasse Archives: page 134 (top left).

✳ Monique Jourdan-Gassin: pages 63, 120 (bottom), 134 (center), 144.

✳ Laziz Hamani/Editions Assouline: pages 7, 8, 9, 11, 13, 20-21, 25, 29, 32, 41, 49, 52–53, 55, 56-57, 59, 69, 72 (bottom right), 75, 81, 85, 91, 95, 97, 107, 113, 115, 123, 139.

✳ Kipa: pages 76–77, still photo from Marcel Pagnol's *Marius*, 1931.

✳ Christian Larit: pages 33, 141.

✳ Fernand Léger/Adagp, Paris 2000: pages 110–111, ceramic, 1952, terrace of La Colombe d'Or (photo by Prosper Assouline/Editions Assouline).

✳ Marcel Loli: page 15.

✳ The Minneapolis Institute of Arts: page 6, *Olive Trees*, Van Gogh, 1889.

✳ Willy Ronis/Rapho: page 120, Le Café de France, L'Isle-sur-la-Sorgue, 1979.

✳ Jean-Yves Salabaj: pages 23, 27, 65.

✳ François Simon: page 87.

✳ Ermel Vialet: pages 17, 22, 35, 37.

✳ All rights reserved: pages 14, 39, 72 (bottom left, Château Romanin, Saint-Rémy-de-Provence).

• Acknowledgments

Many thanks to François Simon for his valuable help, to Céline, Charlotte, Emmanuelle, Ghislaine, Arnaud, Olivier, and Vincent for their proofreading, to Franck Cerutti and Benoît Witz for their "culinary advice," to Dominique Potier, Thierry Blanc, Jérôme di Marino, and the staffs of La Bastide and L'Abbaye for their useful suggestions, to Gérard Margeon and Noël Bajor for the wines of Provence.
Thanks to Gwenaelle, and many thanks, of course, to all those mentioned in this book, the people without whom Provence would not be what it is.

✳ ✳ ✳

The publisher would also like to thank Philippe Caresse, Laziz Hamani, Monique Jourdan-Gassin, Christian Larit, Marcel Loli, Jean-Yves Salabaj, and Ermel Vialet. And, lastly, thanks to Adagp (Paris), to Le Château Romanin, to La Colombe d'Or, Monsieur and Madame Roux, *Cuisine et Vins de France*, Kipa, The Minneapolis Institute of Arts, Rapho, *Terre Provençale*, and all those who participated in the production of the present work.